T0237379

Monitoring Cloud-Native Applications

Lead Agile Operations Confidently Using Open Source Software

Mainak Chakraborty
Ajit Pratap Kundan

Apress®

Monitoring Cloud-Native Applications

Mainak Chakraborty
Gurugram, India

Ajit Pratap Kundan
Faridabad, India

ISBN-13 (pbk): 978-1-4842-6887-2
https://doi.org/10.1007/978-1-4842-6888-9

ISBN-13 (electronic): 978-1-4842-6888-9

Managing Director, Apress Media LLC: Welmoed Spahr
Acquisitions Editor: Aditee Mirashi
Development Editor: Matthew Moodie
Coordinating Editor: Aditee Mirashi

Cover designed by eStudioCalamar

Cover image designed by Freepik (www.freepik.com)

Distributed to the book trade worldwide by Springer Science+Business Media New York, 1 New York Plaza, Suite 4600, New York, NY 10004-1562, USA. Phone 1-800-SPRINGER, fax (201) 348-4505, e-mail orders-ny@ springer-sbm.com, or visit www.springeronline.com. Apress Media, LLC is a California LLC and the sole member (owner) is Springer Science + Business Media Finance Inc (SSBM Finance Inc). SSBM Finance Inc is a **Delaware** corporation.

For information on translations, please e-mail booktranslations@springernature.com; for reprint, paperback, or audio rights, please e-mail bookpermissions@springernature.com.

Apress titles may be purchased in bulk for academic, corporate, or promotional use. eBook versions and licenses are also available for most titles. For more information, reference our Print and eBook Bulk Sales web page at http://www.apress.com/bulk-sales.

Any source code or other supplementary material referenced by the author in this book is available to readers on GitHub via the book's product page, located at www.apress.com/978-1-4842-6887-2. For more detailed information, please visit http://www.apress.com/source-code.

Printed on acid-free paper

To Ritu,
my best friend,
for believing in me.

To Jay Gopal and Gita Chakraborty,
my parents,
for their unwavering support.

—Mainak Chakraborty

Table of Contents

About the Authors

Mainak Chakraborty is a senior solutions architect at a leading public cloud company, specializing in cloud management and automation tools. He has been instrumental in shaping the cloud journey of customers across industry segments whether they be established enterprises or born-in-the-cloud startups. Mainak is an open source enthusiast and regularly presents at industry technical events on his favorite topics of automation, cloud native applications and cloud computing.

Ajit Pratap Kundan stands at the leading edge of the innovative technologies of todays' information technology world. He's worked with companies like HPE, VMware, Novell and helped customers in transforming their datacenters through software-defined services. Ajit is a valued author on cloud technologies and has authored two books—*VMware Cross-Cloud Architecture* and *Intelligent Automation with VMware* published by Packt—and has reviewed one book, *Deep Learning with Pytorch*.

About the Technical Reviewer

 **Amit Agrawal** is a principal data scientist, architect and researcher delivering solutions in the fields of AI and machine learning. He has good experience in designing end-to-end solutions and architecture for enterprise products.

Introduction

When I was growing up, I was very fond of solving puzzles and reading detective stories. I would spend hours scratching my head about hidden treasure troves or solving a murder mystery on a lazy summer afternoon. I would picture myself inside the scene of action trying to catch the culprit red-handed from a vantage point in the attic. The characters would stay with me as I juggled around with the various possible scenarios and their equally plausible outcomes. Sometimes I would deduce the correct answer, mostly when I could see a pattern (or a motive), and be overjoyed with my feat. However, there were times when I would simply fail to come up with any solution and those were the times when I wished I had some superpowers.

Fast-forward to today where I am working on keeping a critical business application alive when suddenly all hell breaks loose. The application is down, customers are not able to access anything and the business is incurring losses by the second. What went wrong?

Don the detective's hat, get your spy glasses, and try to find out the answer. This is similar to searching for the missing necklace from the queen's jewelry box, albeit infinitely more complex. There are many characters involved, some with motives and even some with no motive at all. Finding a pattern or juggling scenarios in your head may not be the right start to your investigations. What you need is a superpower. Voila!

This book is an exercise to provide you with that superpower to accurately find answers to the most critical questions when things start to go haywire with your application. You no longer need to rely on guesswork to find out what went wrong, nor do you need to use trial and error to fix a problem. We will help you get started with the concepts of monitoring, introduce you to popular open source monitoring tools, and help with finding the correct set of use cases for their implementation. The book covers in-depth technical details of open source software used in modern monitoring systems that are tailor-made for environments running microservices.

This book is divided into two parts. Part 1 starts with an introduction to cloud native applications and the foundational concepts of monitoring. It then walks you through the various aspects of monitoring containerized workloads using Kubernetes as the de facto orchestration platform. We will dive deep into the architecture of a modern monitoring system and look at its individual components in detail. Part 2 will introduce you to popular open source tools like Prometheus, TICK Stack, and Grafana, which are used by enterprises and startups alike and are well established as their tools of choice.

After reading this book, you will have a much better understanding of the key terminology and general concepts around observability. You will learn about the complete spectrum of open source monitoring solutions available for applications, microservices and containers and how to quickly reap the benefits. Armed with this knowledge, you will be able to lead day-to-day operations more confidently and be better equipped to navigate the mesh of services sprawling in your environment.

PART I

Architecture of Modern Monitoring Systems for Cloud Native Applications

Modern day systems are dynamic and complicated. They are highly distributed, ephemeral in nature but are built to sustain failure. This change in the underlying design of systems has led to introduction of orchestration platforms like Kubernetes which have abstracted away some of the regular concerns like health-checks, auto-remediation, auto scaling and load-balancing. Rather than looking for individual system behaviour one now must focus on the inter connection of these systems and understand their behaviour as a whole. It becomes necessary to gain better visibility into these systems, in order to learn about the performance of our services in production, which in turn provides with the feedback to build better and robust applications.

In Part 1 of this book, we will introduce you to the two fundamental changes – Microservices and Containers, and their impact on modern software development and resulting application performance. We will talk about monitoring and discuss the impact of modern applications on traditional monitoring, while learning about the various terminologies and roles which have evolved to support this new paradigm of Cloud Native Applications. We would learn about Observability and how is it different from Monitoring and discuss in detail about the 3 pillars of Observability.

We will also look at the individual components of monitoring, understand their functions and how they fit into the overall Modern Monitoring System. We will design an end-to-end architecture that is capable of identification of the minutest problems affecting your systems and then alerting you in the shortest possible time. By the end of Part 1 of this book, the reader will have a solid understanding of monitoring in general, its components and frameworks, the design of what a monitoring system should include and the associated terms and concepts.

CHAPTER 1

Introduction to Modern Monitoring

Digital transformation and cloud computing have changed the IT landscape of several organizations over the course of the last few years. As part of these initiatives, most companies have either already completed or are in the process of migrating their existing applications to the cloud. The reasons for this transition to a cloud-first approach can be attributed to on-demand scalability, pay-per-use model, and easy access to an unfathomably rich set of services previously unviable for organizations with access to limited resources. Garage startups today, even if bootstrapping, have the same platform available to build their business that is powering big commercial enterprises. In fact, many successful startups like Airbnb, Uber, and Netflix took the first-mover advantage of the cloud and are now leaders in their respective segments.

The ongoing shift toward cloud and digital transformation has brought two fundamental changes—one in the field of application development and another in the field of infrastructure. These two significant changes have reshaped the way we interact digitally, for example, making payments using digital payment systems or mobile wallets, using IoT-enabled sensors in our smart homes, or getting a degree from an online classroom program. The efficacy with which these modern applications can handle millions of concurrent transactions today is feasible due to the evolution of the systems running them.

This book is an introductory guide to modern-day monitoring of cloud native applications. It not only covers the technical details of how monitoring solutions work with microservices but also explains in detail the architecture, technical design, and steps for their implementation.

© Mainak Chakraborty and Ajit Pratap Kundan 2021
M. Chakraborty and A. P. Kundan, *Monitoring Cloud-Native Applications*,
https://doi.org/10.1007/978-1-4842-6888-9_1

In this particular chapter, we will introduce you to two fundamental changes in modern software development, the advent of microservices and containers and their impact on application deployment and performance. Then we will talk about monitoring and discuss the influence of modern applications on traditional monitoring. We will also learn about the various terminologies and roles which have evolved to support this new paradigm of cloud native applications. In addition to that, we will look at the various types of monitoring, the difference between reactive and proactive monitoring and the difference between push and pull monitoring. We will also discuss Kubernetes, its various components, and their respective functions. By the end of this chapter, you would have a good overview of modern monitoring and the associated concepts.

Microservices

Traditionally, applications were monolithic in nature. They were built on a single code base and deployed in a three-tier architecture of UI (Web), logic (app), and database (storage). In order to change an existing feature, introduce a new feature, or fix a bug, the complete code would need to be redeployed in production after fixing only that small portion of code which warranted changes. This would usually result in planned downtime for code redeployment, unplanned downtime if the code breaks in production and a massive effort between the development and operations teams to get it off the ground. This would lead to inevitable delays and subsequent revenue loss for the business. In fact, at one time, a release cycle of more than six months was considered as standard in the industry.

As a direct result of digital transformation, businesses today want a quicker release cycle, which would mean rolling out newer features and capturing market share before the competition does. In order to speed up the release cycle, it became obvious to break the single monolithic application code block into smaller chunks of code, which can be worked upon more easily than the entire code base. The application functionality is split into several independent services called microservices, which provide particular functionalities within the overall application.

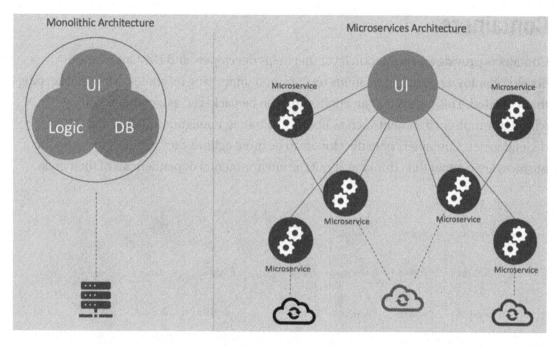

Figure 1-1. *Difference between monolithic and microservices architecture*

For example, imagine your favorite online retailer's website running on monolithic architecture, as seen in Figure 1-1, having inventory management and payment systems in one single code base and deployed on premises. To introduce a change in the inventory management system, it would require changing only the relevant code but deploying the complete application again with downtime, which would result in unhappy customers and lost revenue. In contrast, if it were running on microservices architecture, only the microservice running the inventory management system would need to be modified and redeployed, and the rest of the application would still be accessible. This approach not only provides a newer set of services faster to your end users but also reduces overall downtime.

Microservices is a modern approach to software development that structures an application as a collection of loosely coupled, independently deployable sets of services which are often developed, deployed, and maintained by a single team. This helps in rapid and frequent rollout of features even in a setup running hundreds of such services. Nowadays, born-in-cloud companies have release cycles which can be as frequent as once and even multiple times daily. This means businesses can provide added functionalities faster to their audience and thus generate more revenue or respond faster to customer concerns and therefore retain the existing customer base.

Containers

Containers provide an abstraction layer that helps developers and DevOps teams to develop, deploy, and run applications on common underlying resources, while still keeping them isolated. This means that an application can be packaged as a container along with its runtime environment such as libraries, binaries, configuration files, and other dependencies. Containers help developers to be more agile as they can now focus on the business logic rather than thinking about the environmental dependencies of their code.

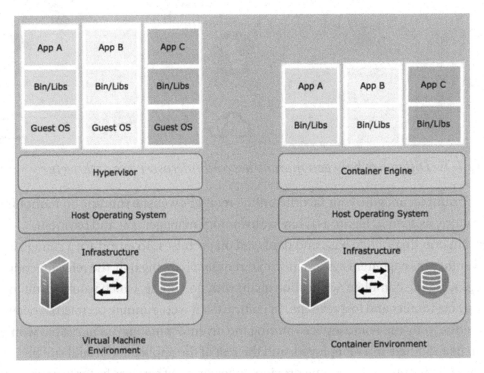

Figure 1-2. *Difference between VMs and containers*

As shown in Figure 1-2, with regards to providing abstraction and isolation, containers closely resemble virtual machines (VMs); however unlike VMs, in a container the application is packaged with only the essential elements for it to run and not the entire guest OS. This allows containers to have unique capabilities when compared with VMs like quick spin-up, minimum overhead, miniscule footprint, and high portability. More and more developers today are consuming cloud-based container services, either managed or unmanaged, to test and deploy their applications. This has given rise to the concept of "cloud native," which is a term that broadly encompasses containerized environments that are run natively in cloud.

As per the Cloud Native Computing Foundation (CNCF):

Cloud native technologies empower organizations to build and run scalable applications in modern, dynamic environments such as public, private, and hybrid clouds. Containers, service meshes, microservices, immutable infra-structure, and declarative APIs exemplify this approach. These techniques enable loosely coupled systems that are resilient, manageable, and observable. Combined with robust automation, they allow engineers to make high-impact changes frequently and predictably with minimal toil.

Containers have been around for some time but have really gained traction now along with the shift to microservices architecture. Companies who want to migrate their workloads easily from one environment to another can rely on containers to provide a logical abstraction of the application from the environment underneath, therefore supporting the use case of easy migration.

Running servers (or VMs) is akin to having pets where each server is given a unique name and taken care of (manually managed). It is of grave concern if one server stops working and all necessary steps are taken to ensure that the server is healthy again (patching, updating, etc.). On the other hand, containers are ephemeral and in contrast to the philosophy of having pets, they are treated as cattle, raised to fulfill certain functions. If they were not to run anymore, nobody would care. They can simply be killed and replaced with another container. The important thing to note here is that containers are created keeping failure scenarios in mind.

A microservices implementation doesn't demand the exclusive use of containers; however, using them is the easiest way to run a microservices architecture on the cloud. Since containers can share resources in the same operating system instance with other application components, they can help in achieving better server utilization rates. Containers also spin up quickly and hence are better suited to respond to increasing demands from erratic workloads. The key attributes of elastic infrastructure and highly distributed application components are fueling the journey toward cloud native. However, these same attributes pose a unique challenge as containers can add significant operational complexity due to their short lifespan and highly dynamic nature. The network flow and routing in between the microservices needs to be configured and controlled.

In scenarios where the number of containers is lower, one can manually perform these operational tasks, but with rapid adoption, the number of containers quickly starts to grow in production and the need for container orchestration starts becoming obvious. Container orchestrators provide management tasks such as resource allocation and management, automation, scaling, health checks, networking, load balancing, and so on. Container orchestration tools like Kubernetes help in automating the deployment, scaling and management of containerized workloads across cloud environments. We will look at Kubernetes in detail later in this chapter.

Monitoring

Monitoring refers to the complete process of gaining visibility and meaningful insight into the state of a system. It includes building a well-defined system of measurement to verify the intended behavior of an entity and quickly notify the administrators involved if there is any drift from that behavior. It helps in identification of the causes of anomalous behavior and rectification of those issues to avoid any potential reoccurrences.

As defined by Rob Ewaschuk in *Site Reliability Engineering: How Google Runs Production Systems* (O'Reilly, 2016):

> *Monitoring means collecting, processing, aggregating and displaying real-time quantitative data about a system, such as query counts and types, error counts and types, processing times, and server lifetimes.*

Importance of Monitoring

Monitoring is important to identify capacity usage and performance trends over a particular time period. It helps in finding the historical utilization of resources, thereby assisting in making informed decisions regarding the future procurement of capacity and it also serves as an input to architectural redesign and most importantly, provides incredible insight into the workings of a system. It is also useful to preemptively discover anomalous behavior before they develop into pesky problems, thereby helping in sustaining availability and maintaining service quality.

Systems emit data either at a regular interval automatically or when an event occurs. By leveraging this data with the help of suitable monitoring systems, we can -

1. Get proactively alerted of potential problems in the system,

2. Quickly analyze and remediate a problem which has already occurred,

3. Determine the overall health of the environment

Therefore, capturing this data is important for the efficient running of your systems and applications. The main use case of monitoring is to timely identify the source of a problem. During an outage, time is of essence, as everyone is geared towards bringing the system up, but there is not much time for a detailed analysis. To resolve this, monitoring systems need to process huge datasets of complex information and present them effectively in easy-to-remember data points. Based on this analysis, operators can then get to the bottom of the problem and rectify it quickly.

The techniques used in modern-day monitoring are varied and cut across the fields of real-time data processing and statistical data analysis. Data visualization also plays an important role, as the processed data must be meaningfully displayed in a human-readable format. There are many ways to interpret data, and monitoring data gives you many different perspectives on the underlying issues from the same dataset.

DevOps—Roles and User Personas

Before the era of DevOps, developers would usually write their code with very little concern for how it will perform in production and push it over the wall to the operations team. The operations team, which was responsible for keeping the application up and running, would invariably point fingers at developers when the code would break in production. DevOps emerged as an answer to resolve this conflict of misaligned priorities between the two groups and proposed a new set of practices to bridge the gap between software development and software operations teams. This evolution of DevOps is depicted in Figure 1-3.

Figure 1-3. *Evolution of DevOps*

To align with the principles of DevOps and Agile methodology, companies have created specific roles within their organizations. One of these roles, which evolved at Google, is that of site reliability engineers (SREs), who are responsible for keeping the systems up and running. SREs monitor their systems for meeting predefined service-level objectives (SLOs) by

- Providing information on system behavior

- Identifying trends of system usage and performance

- Notifying and alerting on outliers and anomalies

- Diagnosing the problem

SREs are tasked with the reliability of the production system and therefore need to have a solid understanding of the services running in production and how are they being monitored. If unarmed with proper tools and information, SREs won't be able to quickly locate important information even after identifying abnormal behavior. Figure 1-4 shows the five pillars of DevOps and their corresponding SRE practices:

Five Pillars of DevOps	DevOps	SRE
Collaborative Culture	DevOps focuses on reducing silos between Dev and Ops teams	SREs focus on working with developers to resolve issues by sharing the same tools
Lean	Systems are built for failure and failure mechanisms are well thought through	Use different rollout mechanisms to balance between availability and failures for every new release
Measurement	Measure everything through carefully defined instrumentation	Define prescriptive ways for measuring availability, uptime, and outages
Automation	DevOps encourages automation using tools to reduce hard-coded manual work	Focuses on value addition to the system by minimizing manual tasks
Cultural Change	Preaches gradual change in the current processes	Encourages change to reduce costs of failure

Figure 1-4. Five pillars of DevOps

Monitoring Domains

Environments differ in scope and in the mechanisms with which they can be monitored. Different roles within an organization are responsible for monitoring different areas related to an application and hence they design and instrument these for different priorities, which can be broadly classified as seen in Figure 1-5:

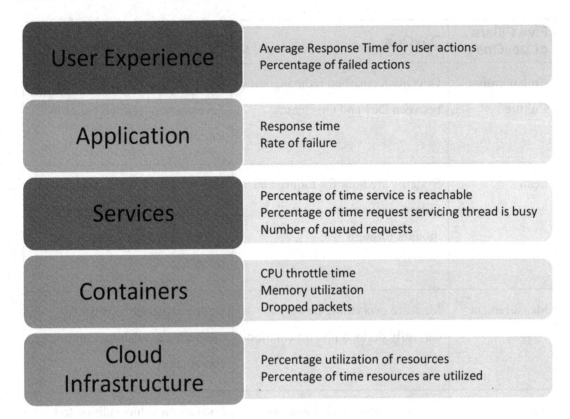

Figure 1-5. *Monitoring domains*

Let us explore these domains, as seen in Figure 1-5, from the cloud infrastructure layer and work our way to the top of the monitoring pyramid.

> **Cloud infrastructure:** Cloud admins, system admins, operations teams are interested in the utilization of resources in cloud be it CPU, memory, network, or storage. They monitor the utilization patterns over time to figure out if the resources are being over- or underutilized. They are also interested in knowing whether the change in utilization is expected behavior, and if not, what it can be attributed to (e.g., unexpected rise in demand or a new feature rollout that peaked the memory utilization levels, etc.). In addition to that, utilization trends are a good indicator of future capacity demands and can help in figuring out the capacity to be procured and the associated costs beforehand.

Containers: SREs are tasked with ensuring the availability of containers. SREs monitor the containers for specific utilization parameters as well as the processes running inside the containers. This information can help in refining the design of the system by introducing a queueing mechanism in place to ensure that requests don't need to be rate limited. Some of the indicators can be the uptime percentage of the container, how many requests are in queue, or the average percentage of time a request servicing thread is busy. Container performance is not an isolated activity; rather, it is relevant in tracking the performance of the cloud infrastructure on which they are deployed and the applications they run.

Services: A service is an abstraction of an application, forming part of a microservice, running in containers that can be traced across multiple clusters. Tracking services for health and performance information is akin to looking at application components for application performance and latency. The mechanism that allows a client to find and access its dependent services is called service discovery. The process of distributing the incoming requests across the set of instances is called dynamic routing. Service meshes place priority on health information over the proximity of service when it comes to determining whether to route traffic to an instance or not.

Applications: Developers and DevOps admins care more about the response time and failure rate, which can be either of a single service within an application or of the application as a whole. They are concerned about how the database responds, how many queries it responds to in a minute, the change of heap memory usage over time, and so on. This information is relevant for the developers to continuously improve their application over time, resulting in a better user experience.

User Experience: Web analytics is a specialized field of monitoring user behavior, which is important to understand how users interact with the application, what keeps them engaged, and how are they using the services offered by the application.

Clickstream monitoring refers to the tracking of user visits to websites using web server log files. It is useful to measure the stickiness of a user, user behavior, and the location of access, which helps in running digital marketing and targeted advertising campaigns. Companies are interested in information such as the average time each user spends on their web/mobile application and how many users are new users vs. returning users. User experience data can include page load time, mobile crash information, JavaScript errors, and the like. Synthetic monitoring is another popular technique to monitor applications by simulating user behavior inside the application. User experience is the single most important factor that drives customer satisfaction and therefore the business outcomes.

Business KPI (Key Performance Indicators): In the past, developers were generally responsible for the technology stack and the operations team for application uptime, but neither were responsible for the corresponding business impact. However, with DevOps, more and more teams are now focusing on quantifying the business impact, since it serves as an important feedback about new feature rollouts, most importantly, whether they have succeeded or failed. This can help orient organizational initiatives to tap into other areas with more business potential. Adding business KPI monitoring does serve as a good checkpoint to track whether your applications are delivering value to your customers or not. KPI can include number of mobile app launches, end-to-end user story from login to purchase, revenue processing, impressions and ad-clicks, all of which are important measures for business teams to identify areas that are doing well and rectify those that aren't.

Now we understood the domains in which monitoring is possible, the scope of what can be monitored, and the implications of the monitored data. An important thing to note here is that monitoring isn't limited to the domains mentioned earlier but can be extended to other areas as well.

Reactive vs. Proactive Monitoring

Until a few years ago, organizations would deploy tools such as Nagios and Graphite to reactively do basic checks of CPU, memory, and storage for investigating parameters like capacity utilization and performance. The focus was on measuring availability and managing IT assets. There was very little scope of measuring customer experience, quality of service, and so on; rather, the main focus was to help IT keep the lights on. This type of passive monitoring is termed as reactive monitoring and is managed singularly by the operations team.

Reactive monitoring is primarily concerned with generating infrastructure-centric monitoring data to inform if a node is down, a service is not reachable, so on and so forth. This data is not suitable for making business decisions and doesn't provide application developers with the insight they would need to enhance their applications and improve performance. This data only serves the purposes of its creators—the operations team. It is therefore reasonable that other teams feel disassociated from the performance and availability parameters of the infrastructure and applications being monitored. With no proper insight, developers don't feel accountable for issues and faults with the environment.

This problem is fixed by proactive monitoring, which is considered central to managing cloud infrastructure, modern applications, and digital businesses. Proactive monitoring is automatic as applications are instrumented during the development process itself to generate useful information that can be monitored. It tends to place an application at the center of its universe, focusing on measuring application performance and associated business outcomes rather than basic CPU and memory checks. As part of the monitoring process, performance data is collected and used frequently for analysis and fault resolution along with alerts that are annotated with context and integrated with notification and incident management systems. There is a focus on measuring quality of service and customer experience. This data is relevant to the business teams, product engineering teams, and DevOps teams, as they usually build dashboards and reports based on this data for recording their SLOs. Monitoring is managed by SREs but the responsibility for ensuring that new applications and services are performing as expected is delegated to application developers. New products or releases are not considered feature complete or ready for deployment without adding monitoring to the standard operating procedure.

Monitoring System

A monitoring system is a collection of several different modules that help with the data collection, processing, storage, and visualization to gain remarkable insights into the availability and performance of applications, services, and infrastructure. There are several monitoring systems available in the monitoring universe, out of which some are open source. Figure 1-6 lists the prominent monitoring systems[1] from which we will cover the most popular open source ones in Part 2 of this book.

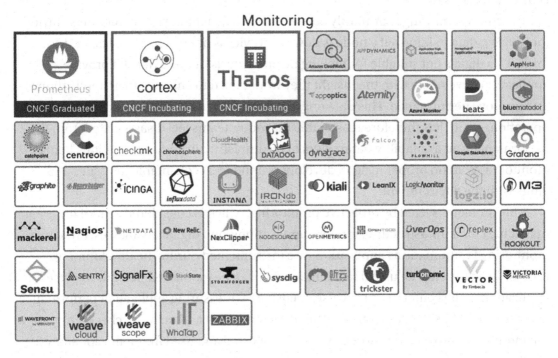

Figure 1-6. *Leading monitoring systems*

Need for a Monitoring System

In the earlier sections, we learned about the importance of monitoring and in this section, we will look at the need for a monitoring system. There are several use cases for which most organizations would use a monitoring system, some of which are detailed as follows:

---

[1]Grayed-out logos are not open source. Source: `https://landscape.cncf.io/`. Licensed under the Apache License 2.0.

- **Detecting problems early:** The goal of an effective monitoring system is to quickly identify a problem. It can be difficult when there are moving parts to a problem in a dynamic environment and the objective is to figure out the actual reason for an outage as quickly as possible. This is where an effective monitoring system helps us by quickly identifying that a threshold has been breached and notifying the relevant administrators so that the problem can be looked into and resolved.

- **Ensuring availability:** Availability is an important SLO for SREs, and it refers to reducing the downtime as much as possible. Downtime means that there is partial or complete unavailability of the application for end user, which can also mean loss of business revenue and customer satisfaction. In general, this is the single most important criterion which organizations try to avoid by deploying a monitoring system. If configured properly, a monitoring system can preemptively let you know the areas having a high probability to get impacted in future, by a careful study of the data received from your system. This data is commonly used for the predictive maintenance of your systems. Also, with the use of AI/ML, some systems can go into a self-healing mode and automatically rectify the problem. Refer to the last section in this chapter, where we briefly talk about AI-based operations (AIOps) and Operations as a Code.

- **Measuring performance:** The goal of an effective monitoring system is to help developers improve application performance over time. This can only be done when they can visualize the performance trends and patterns to figure out the areas that need to be investigated. For example, by analyzing the storage I/O patterns over time, we can understand the behavior of the application during different times of the day or during promotional events.

A monitoring system is not an isolated setup only for the operations teams and the SREs to manage. The benefits of any monitoring system are more pronounced when infrastructure teams, product engineering teams, application developers, and operations teams collaborate, exchange observations, and assign areas of responsibilities. A single point of reference for all teams significantly boosts the efficacy of the entire system by detecting and mitigating problems quickly.

Features of a Modern Monitoring System

- **Aggregation using tags/labels:** Tagging or labeling the data your workloads generate adds rich context, making them more insightfull into the working of your systems. This helps the operations teams to slice and dice monitoring data based on these labels, which helps in aggregating the data on a service level rather than on an individual per-system level. In modern monitoring, information pertaining to a single host is of no use as distributed systems are comprised of several hosts. Since SREs are most interested in SLOs, it makes more sense to aggregate the data on a per-service level, to understand whether a service meets its SLOs or not even when one or more individual components may not be working.

- **Collect data from everywhere:** Collecting all the information available from within the system helps SREs to correlate them across all the components involved. For example, for identifying why there is latency associated with a particular service, it is imperative to collate data from the application, containers, underlying hardware, and so forth and then correlate it to understand the complete picture. In some cases, the data from dependent upstream or downstream services might also need to be analyzed for an in-depth investigation of the root causes of any inexplicable behavior.

- **Collaboration:** In a distributed architecture, services are loosely coupled (i.e., services have some components that are dependent on another service developed and managed by another team). It becomes very important that the teams collaborate with each other in order to pinpoint the source of a problem and quickly rectify it. They should also have access to a common communication channel like Slack and should be able to share dashboards with each other. For example, if a database query is taking a long time to complete, SRE will collect the data related to DB query response time, put the information in a dashboard, and share it with a database administrator for review.

- **Auto-notification:** Monitoring tools fire alerts and notify admins when a metric crosses a defined threshold limit. This works for static systems, but in dynamic environments, thresholds need to be modified and tuned constantly. Advanced monitoring systems offer flexible alerting that can modify these thresholds to reflect the changing baselines, using AIOps. They also include features like relative change alerts, automated outliers, and anomaly detection.

- **Discovery:** In cloud computing, resources are added on the fly based on demand. If you configured your monitoring system to only monitor those resources which were present initially, most likely you are not capturing the telemetry data from the new resources provisioned as a result of autoscaling. Modern monitoring systems are able to automatically detect the new resources and can bring them under their gambit for monitoring. When the service is deprecated, the monitoring system automatically stops collecting the data.

Traditional monitoring was restricted to the monitoring of individual systems like application servers, database servers, and so on. Monitoring systems would collect data for basic checks like availability, utilization, and performance. This data would then be fed to static widgets in predefined dashboards in a central console to oversee the monitoring of the complete IT environment. This single view from multiple individual systems was totally unrelated and the possibility to do correlation was at best a guesswork. These monitoring systems were built to ensure availability, reduce downtime, and efficiently manage individual IT assets only.

In the past, monitoring was inherently reactive and centered around predictable faults and plausible human interventions. Administrators would try to foresee what could go wrong and monitor around those aspects. They would also build alerting mechanisms for those parameters which could be rectified quickly with human intervention. These monitoring systems were built for success, assuming systems would always be available, and any change was done only as an afterthought, in response to outages.

Modern-day systems are more dynamic and complicated. These systems are highly distributed, ephemeral, and built to sustain failure. This change in the underlying design of systems has led to the introduction of orchestration platforms like Kubernetes, which have abstracted away some of the regular concerns like health checks, autoremediation, autoscaling, and load balancing. Rather than looking for individual system behavior one now must focus on the interconnection of these systems and understand their interaction with each other. It therefore becomes necessary to gain better visibility into these systems in order to learn about the performance of our services in production, which in turn provides feedback to build better and robust applications.

Push vs. Pull Monitoring

In traditional monitoring systems, there was a central component which used to poll the system for availability data, sitting outside of the system. This used to work while there were a finite number of systems that had to be polled. When the number of systems and services begin to grow, the central component had to be scaled up in order to cater to the growing demand. This could go on for a couple of months or years, after which the entire monitoring system would have to be redesigned. Operations teams ended up spending more time dedicatedly managing their monitoring systems than managing business-critical applications and the underlying infrastructure which was their primary objective.

Quite a few monitoring systems rely on pull-based polling mechanisms of monitoring even today. These systems send a query to the components being monitored to check for availability. This works well while there are a limited number of components that need to be queried. The more hosts and services you add into the mix, the more the monitoring environment would need to be scaled up. With a push-based architecture, all components—whether they be hosts, services, or applications—send data to a central collector. The collection is fully distributed on the hosts, services, and applications that emit data. This means monitoring is no longer a monolithic central function, and we don't need to vertically scale or partition that monolith as and when more end points are added.

In a push model, the components pushing data are called emitters. They send data when it is available and as soon as it is generated. They can use transport mechanisms of their choice to send data, rather than being forced into a specific choice by the monitoring tools. This enables us to build modular, functionally isolated, effective monitoring solutions rather than monolithic silos.

In a pull-based architecture, targets which are to be monitored are centrally configured first for what needs to be monitored; in a push-based architecture, however, the monitoring targets push data to destinations you've configured. This is relevant in a dynamic environment where a short-lived activity might not be discovered automatically into configuration by a pull-based monitor. With a push-based architecture, this is not an issue as the emitter controls when and where the data is sent.

Pull-based monitoring systems generally emphasize monitoring availability and reducing downtime. They focus on point-specific availability alerts, for example, an Apache server has stopped working. Solving these issues can be hugely attractive, because it is often much easier and faster than addressing more systemic issues, such as a 5% increase in HTTP 500 errors. However, focusing toward availability, rather than quality and service, treats IT as simply assets that need to be managed. Therefore, we now need to measure the quality and performance of IT assets and not just their availability. Performance and service quality data is crucial to both business and technology teams for making good decisions.

Push-based monitoring systems are better suited to measure the contextual information of components and services for performance parameters. As collection is distributed and generally has low overhead, you can push a lot of data and store it with high precision as well. This increased precision of data can then be used to more quickly answer questions about quality of service, performance, and availability which orients the focus toward measuring throughput and latency performance.

Advent of AIOps

AIOps is a very nascent area which is gathering traction in the field of monitoring. DevOps teams can harness the power of Artificial Intelligence (AI) and Machine Learning (ML) to identify, prevent, and respond to problems faster and more accurately. It uses AI and ML to analyze the system-generated data to predict possible problems, determine the root causes, and drive automation to fix them. AIOps can also complement the value you get from monitoring by providing an intelligent feed of information from past incidents alongside your monitoring data. AIOps helps in four main ways:

- Reduction in noise to help SREs prioritize alerts and focus on the critical issues that matter most, by correlating related incidents

- Proactive detection of anomalies before an issue hits production and results in negative customer experience

- Intelligent alerting and escalation to automatically route incidents to the individuals or teams best equipped to respond

- Automated incident remediation, which includes workflows to resolve the incident when it occurs and reduce mean time to resolution (MTTR)

Kubernetes

Kubernetes was originally developed at Google from their internal container management platform, Borg; the lessons learned from running Borg in production influenced Kubernetes heavily. Google used to run 2 billion containers a week, and in order to run such a massive environment, they used declarative constructs, which defines the eventual consistency of a system and let the orchestrator achieve it on its own. This design is both repeatable and easily upgradable, and is basically a "set once and then forget" notion of running modern systems.

Kubernetes is the first graduated CNCF project, which is now a popular industry standard open source container orchestration platform that manages the complexities of containerized applications. Its main purpose is to track container utilization, scale based on utilization, continuously check the health, load balance, and automatically self-heal by restarting the containers, if needed. Kubernetes can be run on public clouds or consumed as a managed service from all the leading cloud providers.

We are discussing Kubernetes in this book because it has become the mainstay for running container clusters on which your microservices-based application will be deployed. All throughout the book, we will not only deploy applications, but our monitoring systems also, on top of Kubernetes clusters. Therefore, it is pertinent to quickly glance through the components of Kubernetes and understand their function before we start using them in the next chapters. Please note that this section is not intended as a Kubernetes primer or learning guide.

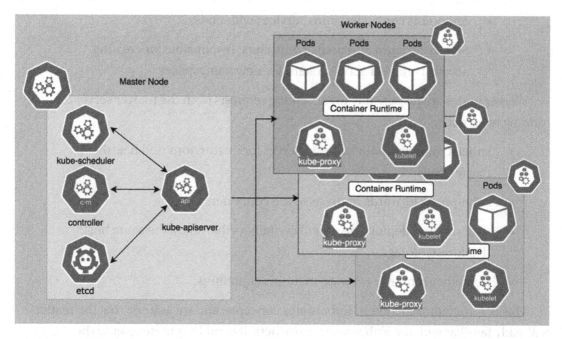

Figure 1-7. *Kubernetes architecture*

Figure 1-7 shows the architecture of the individual components within a Kubernetes cluster. Master node is the single central unit of the cluster which does the management, planning, scheduling, and monitoring of the several worker nodes and runs the following components as containers:

- kube-apiserver: front end for control plane; manages and orchestrates everything on the master node

- etcd: key/value datastore which has the metadata of which containers are running on which worker nodes

- kube-scheduler: responsible for deciding which containers go into which worker nodes

- kube-controller-manager: regulates the state of the cluster by running controller processes, such as

  - Node controller: responsible for tracking node status

  - Replication controller: responsible for maintaining exact number of pods

23

- Endpoints controller: joins services with pods

- Service account and token controllers: responsible for creating account and API access tokens for new namespaces

Worker nodes are responsible for accepting requests from the master server and running workloads:

- kubelet: interacts with kube-apiserver for instructions and heartbeat, creates pods

- kube-proxy: forwards requests to the containers

- Pod: smallest deployable unit of containers that share the same host, IP address, storage

- Container runtime: software that runs containers

This is a brief introduction to Kubernetes concepts, and we assume that the reader is already familiar with the Kubernetes constructs. If need be, please refer to the documentation available at `www.kubernetes.io` before moving on to the next chapters.

Summary

In this chapter, we looked at the dynamic world of cloud native applications, where we learned about microservices and containers and how they are impacting the field of modern application development. We also discussed monitoring in general and how it has evolved over time with the advent of DevOps. We then discussed monitoring systems and looked at the container orchestration platform, Kubernetes. This chapter should have given the reader an overview of the modern monitoring world. In the next chapter, we will build on the concepts of monitoring learned in this chapter to introduce the reader to observability and discuss how is it different from monitoring. We will also dive deep into the three pillars of observability: metrics, logs, and traces.

## CHAPTER 2

Observability

When environments are as complex as they are today, simply monitoring for known problems doesn't address the growing number of new issues that arise as services scale to meet demands. It is fairly difficult to ascertain from the beginning about what can go wrong. In most scenarios, the standard tooling is not good enough to even start the analysis. By the time one starts, systems would have already changed with fluctuating demand patterns and sometimes new systems would have appeared in place of old ones. This escalating complexity is why observability is necessary to build and run today's on-demand cloud native applications. The focus gained by observability with the operations teams is a testament to its effectiveness at enabling IT teams to deliver excellent customer experience in spite of the complexity of underlying resources and systems.

In this chapter, we will learn about observability and how is it different from monitoring. We will also discuss in detail about the three pillars of observability and their importance. In addition to that, we will explore how to extend the learnings from observability to Kubernetes clusters. By the end of this chapter, the reader should have a good understanding of the concepts of observability and how they can be applied to Kubernetes clusters running cloud native workloads.

Observability

Observability is a concept borrowed from Control Theory that focuses on the study of interpreting the internal workings of a system from the external parameters available from the system. It is defined as a mechanism to collect every piece of information about the system, by instrumenting it for granular insightful data, in order to reconstruct a complete picture of the system's internal status in real time. It provides context-rich data that can help us gain visibility into the not-so-explicit failures and then debug them with the use of available information. It focuses on answering those set of questions which haven't been formulated prior to deploying the system in production.

© Mainak Chakraborty and Ajit Pratap Kundan 2021
M. Chakraborty and A. P. Kundan, *Monitoring Cloud-Native Applications*,
https://doi.org/10.1007/978-1-4842-6888-9_2

There are two major objectives of an observability platform. The first one is to identify the baseline performance. Once the baseline performance is identified, developers would want to improve it in order to increase customer satisfaction or user experience. The second objective is to restore the baseline performance in case an issue starts impacting user experience. Observability is about generating that useful set of information which is required while debugging in production. Since we are still not at a point where tools can automatically resolve 100% of the issues, observability can help narrow down the areas which needs to be investigated.

Three Pillars of Observability

Metrics (along with events), logs, and traces are popularly termed as the three pillars of observability. By combining these three together, observability addresses the challenges of monitoring cloud native applications in highly distributed environments. In this section, we will learn about these pillars in detail.

Metrics is the foundational pillar of observability, as it is easiest to collect and cheapest to store. Metrics are numerical, and therefore it is easy to run analysis on them. They can be labeled for a particular dimension or an attribute and when aggregated can present multiple dimensions of the overall system health. There are several ways to collect metrics, prominent amongst which are code instrumentation for collecting metrics from applications or running an agent for collecting metrics from infrastructure. There are several popular open source tools that can help in metric collection, such as Prometheus, StatsD, and Telegraf. We will cover metrics and their types in detail in this chapter and metrics collection and storage in detail in chapter 3.

Measurements that are gathered at regular time intervals (2,4,6,8,10,12) are called metrics, and those measurements that are gathered at irregular time intervals (2,3,6,7,10,11,12) are called events (Figure 2-1).

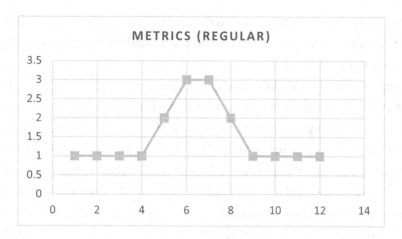

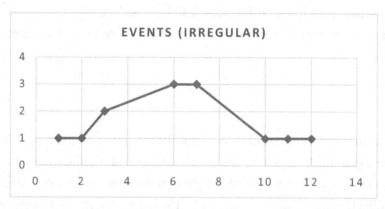

Figure 2-1. *Metrics and events*

Events are another important sub-pillar which is usually clubbed with metrics but should definitely be a part of any sound observability strategy. The difference between metrics and events is that metrics are collected at a regular time interval whereas events are a record of significant occurrences from the same system under observation. Events such as alerts getting triggered, deployment failures, and transaction completions are all important happenings taking place at irregular time intervals. Events contain metadata to sharpen the context and provides the ability to perform real-time fine-grained analysis.

Logs are detailed journals of everything that has happened within a system in a structured text format and are crucial for performing root cause analysis. They can help in recreating the past, as these are comprehensive records providing high-fidelity data and detailed context around an occurrence. Logs are either printed out as events occur or stored for future analysis. While there are standard schemas for logs (as in the case of web server logs), the log structure can also depend on the application. Similar to metrics, there are several open source tools that can help with collecting and storing logs, such as Fluentd and Logstash.

Traces help us to understand the latency of transactions in between the distributed systems as they communicate with each other using remote procedural calls (RPCs) in response to a request. They combine the individual transactions into a logical request called trace, which can give us insight into the customer journey as they interact with various services in our distributed system. Traces enable SREs to understand these journeys, find bottlenecks, and identify latencies that can be fixed or optimized.

These three pillars are interconnected and though you can use one or more than one of these to solve problems, an observability platform requires that these three pillars work in tandem to produce the desired results. Metrics can be used to identify a subset of traces that seem to be problematic and logs associated with those traces can help in finding the root cause. New metrics can be configured to catch the same issue earlier next time.

Metrics

Metrics are the numerical representation of monitored data at a given point in time collected from a system. A sequence of metrics collected at regular intervals, over a period of time, can provide meaningful insight into the state of a system. Since numeric data can be collected, processed, stored, and retrieved easily, metrics provide an efficient way to reflect useful trends in dashboards.

Metrics provide a dynamic, real-time picture of the state and performance of the system that is being monitored. With the help of anomaly detection and analysis of patterns, metrics can help in finding faults proactively before an actual outage takes place.

Metrics are also well suited for the reduction of data resolution over time, aggregating the collected data into daily/weekly frequency as it starts getting old. For example, if you had originally collected 50 metric points per second, throughout the day for a week you can aggregate these over a week, resulting in reduced data granularity but also saving storage space, especially if this data is few months old and no specific issue was highlighted that week.

Each metric consists of some measurement called data value, a timestamp at which the measurement was recorded, and a set of tags and labels to describe the metric.

When these timestamps are aggregated over a fixed time interval and the trendline of the measurement is plotted in a two-dimensional plot of data value vs. time, it yields meaningful insights, using context from tags, to arrive at a conclusion.

Time Series

Metrics provides us with a point-in-time observation of a particular parameter and its corresponding value. The collection of these point-in-time observations when spaced over equal time intervals is called time series. It helps us identify an outlier in the series of observations and also understand the underlying reason for that outlier. Since the data in a time series is essentially a numeric value, it is appropriate to work out a model for forecasting and statistical analysis. Time series is an important concept which underlines most modern monitoring systems. We will discuss time series and time-series databases in more detail in chapter 3.

Granularity/Resolution

Metrics are generally collected at a fixed time interval which is known as the granularity or resolution. It can range from a second to several minutes. It is important to find the granularity needed to effectively observe the behavior of your system. If you select a fine granularity of 1 second, you could end up polling the system too frequently, which may lead up to a phenomenon called observer effect, which negatively impacts the performance of your systems. Too many data points can also result in large storage consumption and the data might not vary as much within a period of a few seconds. On the other hand, if you a select coarse granularity of several minutes, you might end up losing valuable information between the selected time interval. This can defeat the purpose of collecting the metrics.

Therefore, an effective strategy is to have different levels of granularity for different components of a system. For example, in the case of storage utilization, a fine granularity of a few seconds is important to determine the disk I/Os because a minute-long granularity will not reveal the quieter short-lived spikes that drive high tail latencies in applications. Tail latency refers to the percentage of responses which takes the longest to complete when compared to the overall responses served by the system. For example, if the system on an average has a response time of 5 ms and the 99th percentile of requests are fulfilled within 5 ms, then the remaining responses which are taking more than 5 ms need to be investigated. Some of these responses might even take as long as 1 second, which is a cause for concern and reflects high tail latency.

Metadata Tags

Monitoring cloud native environments, which are always in flux, is very challenging. The methods and processes applied for traditional monitoring systems are not suitable for these dynamic environments. Even if they can monitor subsystems, they lack context and aren't capable of scaling sufficiently to meet the challenges of an ever-growing mesh of interconnected services running an application.

Tags are the cornerstone of observability, as they allow us to aggregate information across the complete environment without modifying the way in which metrics are collected. Tags are metadata that adds context to a metric. Once tags are added to metrics, it is easier to reconfigure collected data, club all metrics from a set of related services, or alert on metrics from different services. This mechanism helps in shifting the focus from monitoring individual resources like OS and servers to monitoring the latency of a single service or the availability of the entire application.

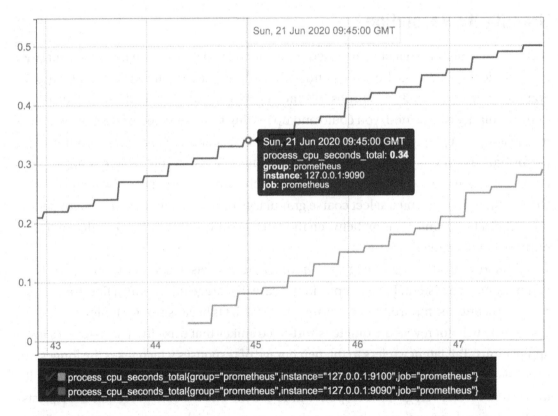

Figure 2-2. *Tags and labels*

Figure 2-2 depicts a chart for a metric process_cpu_seconds_total. The measurement here includes a timestamp - Sun, 21 Jun 2020 09:45:00 GMT, a metric name - process_cpu_seconds_total, a metric value - 0.34, and some labels such as group: prometheus, instance: 127.0.0.1:9090 and job: prometheus. Figure 2-3 shows the components of a metric.

Metric Name	Metric Value	Timestamp	Tags
process_cpu_seconds_total	0.34	Sun, 21 Jun 2020 09:45:00 GMT	group: prometheus instance: 127.0.0.1:9090 job: prometheus

Figure 2-3. *Components of a metric*

Tags are also commonly known as labels and are generally represented as key/value pairs, where key adds a particular context to the metric and its corresponding value becomes an attribute for that context. "key" is the dimension that you assign to a metric (e.g., instance), and the "value" determines the data for that dimension (e.g., metrics from instance - 127.0.0.1:9090). Now for the same "key"="instance," other instances with different values (e.g., 127.0.0.1:9100) can be grouped together. Once these tags are added, monitored data can then be sliced and diced across any dimension.

Tags decouple the process of data collection and reporting. In case tags were not added, then metrics for each instance from the preceding example would have to be hard-coded as process_cpu_seconds_total.prometheus.127.0.0.1:9090, which will be very cumbersome to work with since developers would have to exactly pinpoint the instance where their code will run. This is practically impossible in a distributed environment. Also, if another dimension were to be added, the metric would need to be updated accordingly for additional scope and the code must be instrumented likewise. In a containerized environment, doing this is simply not feasible. With tags, there is no need to preconfigure anything; only the key is sufficient to aggregate the values together.

Categories of Metrics

Metrics can be broadly classified as work metrics or resource metrics depending on the information the metric delivers. Work metrics deliver information about the output of the whole system or its subsystems. Resource metrics provide information about the resources that make up the whole system or its subsystems. Work metrics are focused on overall system behavior, whereas resource metrics are concerned with the behavior of the individual resources that are part of that system. Work metrics include throughput, success, errors, and latency, whereas resource metrics include errors, saturation, utilization, and availability. Work and resource metrics together can help you easily visualize the health of your services and diagnose for problems. Let's learn about each of these in detail:

Work Metrics

Throughput: An absolute measure of the amount of work done by a component per unit of time. In the case of an application, throughput is the measure of the number of concurrent processes managed per second. Similarly, for a database, it is the number of queries executed per second. In the case of a web server, throughput would be the number of HTTP requests processed per second. It helps in quantifying the demand that is placed on the system.

Success: A measure of the rate of requests that resulted in success per unit of time.

Error: A measure of the rate of requests that resulted in errors per unit of time. It can also be measured as errors per unit of work when normalized by the throughput. Error metrics are often captured for all potential sources that can generate errors in order to track and accordingly take action on them. Protocol response code can be insufficient in covering all failure scenarios; hence, other secondary protocols might be necessary to cover the partial failure cases.

Latency: Latency is a measure of the time required to complete a unit of work. It is recommended to measure latency for all requests, whether resulting in success or failure. Latency for transactions that resulted in an error is often useful in tracking the problem. It can be expressed as an average or a percentile, such as 97% of requests were returned within 0.5 seconds.

Sample work metrics for web server:

Subtype	Description	Value
Throughput	HTTP requests per second	6590
Success	percentage of 2xx responses	99.2
Error	percentage of 5xx responses	0.5
Latency	97th-percentile response time in seconds	0.1

Sample work metrics for database server:

Subtype	Description	Value
Throughput	queries executed per second	712
Success	percentage of queries successfully executed	100
Error	percentage of queries yielding exceptions	0
Latency	95th-percentile query time in seconds	0.02

Resource Metrics

Saturation: Saturation is a measure of the load that a service is able to take but cannot service yet, or in other words, saturation defines how full a service is. It is a measure of the resources that are most constrained; for example, saturation will let you know if a service can properly handle double the traffic without service degradation. Latency increases are often an indicator of saturation. If you measure your 99th-percentile response time over a period of 1 minute, it might show an early signal of saturation.

Utilization: Utilization is a measure of the resource capacity that is under use. It is calculated as a percentage of time that the resource is busy.

Errors: Errors represent internal system errors that may not be observable in the output the resource produces.

Availability: Availability is a simple check of resources available for work to be done and is represented as the percentage of time that these resources respond to the requests.

Sample resource metrics of common resources:

Resource	Saturation	Utilization	Errors	Availability
Microservice	# enqueued requests	average % time each request-servicing thread was busy	# internal errors, exceptions	% of time service is reachable
Memory	swap usage	% of total memory in use	-	-
Database	# enqueued queries	average % of time each connection was found busy	# internal errors, replication errors	% of time database is reachable
Disk I/O	wait queue length	% of time that device was busy	# device errors	% of time disk is writable

Now we understand that metrics can be associated with the workload/application (work metrics) or the resources that drive that workload (resource metrics). It is important to observe and track work metrics, as they have a direct bearing on customer satisfaction, whereas monitoring resource metrics is also crucial, as they impact the work metrics directly and therefore have an implication on the user experience.

Methods of Measurement

USE Method[1]

The Utilization, Saturation, and Errors (USE) methodology is used for analyzing system performance by measuring utilization, saturation, and errors of system resources, such as memory utilization, CPU run queue length (saturation), and device errors. Once the capacity of a resource reaches 100% utilization, it either queues the work (saturation) or

---

[1]Coined by Brendan Gregg

returns errors which are also identified using the USE method. Since the USE method focuses on fewer but key metrics, all the system resources are quickly checked. The USE metrics are usually expressed as follows:

- **Utilization:** As a percentage; for example, CPU is at 90% utilization

- **Saturation:** As a wait-queue length,;for example, CPUs have an average run queue length of four

- **Errors:** As the number of errors reported; for example, the network interface had 50 late collisions

Errors are critical because they can degrade performance and may not be immediately noticeable. For example, operations that fail and are retried and systems that fail in a pool of redundant systems can go unnoticed and hide potentially bigger problems. Errors are placed first before utilization and saturation are checked, and it can save crucial time if they are investigated first before the other metrics.

It is interesting to note that a short spike in utilization can cause saturation and performance issues, even though the overall utilization over a long time period, say 5 minutes, may remain low. Some monitoring tools report utilization over 5-minute averages, which will cause this spike to go unnoticed. CPU utilization, for example, can fluctuate drastically from second to second, so a 5-minute average may disguise short periods of 100% utilization and therefore saturation. The USE method may not be the ideal fit for these use cases. The USE approach has its limitations with the infrastructure-focused approach. For instance, it is difficult to measure the saturation of memory, or the amount of memory used. Also, error counts can be problematic, especially I/O errors and memory bandwidth. There is another popular method called the RED method, which takes a different approach to look at the preceding problems.

RED Method[2]

The RED method as depicted in the Figure 2-4 monitors the request rate (R), error rate (E), and duration of request (D), which are necessary for monitoring request-driven, application-level metrics. The most immediate benefit to instrumenting microservices by using RED method is to give developers a standard set of tools to diagnose and rectify an issue.

---

[2]Coined by Tom Wilkie

Request rate: This is the rate at which the incoming requests are measured on a per-second basis. In the case of a web application, the request rate would correspond to the count of HTTP requests received per second. HTTP requests can be too frequent, so it's always better to focus on request rate change rather than simply request rate. For example, if a webpage that normally generates 25 HTTP requests suddenly sees the request rate jump to 50, this would indicate that something unusual has happened. We can now investigate to find out what those additional requests are to understand the sudden surge.

Error: With the number of requests at our disposal, we can now check how many of these requests are succeeding or failing. Error metric is a count of the number of requests that have failed. In the case of a web application, this will be the count of HTTP requests that return status codes like 400s or 500s. If you are seeing a lot of 501 responses from your HA proxy, it's a clear indication of something not working correctly.

Duration: It is also equally important to consider how long it takes for the user to get a response. Duration is the amount of time it takes for a request to be processed. The last thing a user wants is to wait longer for a response than the usual. If the duration is significantly higher than normally expected, it indicates some problem with the system, usually latency or saturation.

Figure 2-4. *RED method*

It is recommended to use the USE and RED methods together, as the RED method talks about the parameters that impacts users, whereas the USE method talks about parameters impacting the system. These are two complimentary perspectives on the same environment.

Four Golden Signals

The four golden signals of monitoring are latency, traffic, errors, and saturation, which was first propounded in *Site Reliability Engineering: How Google Runs Production Systems* (O'Reilly, 2016). In Figure 2-5, these four golden signals are depicted and each one of these signals has a direct impact on customer experience.

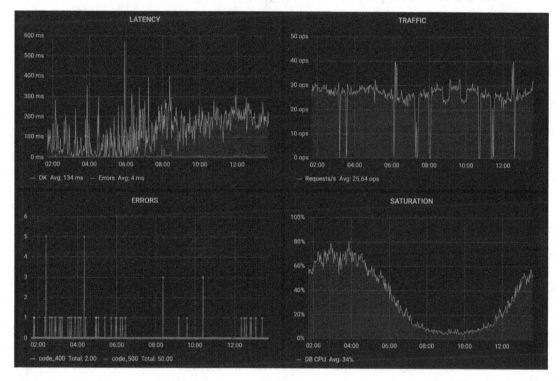

Figure 2-5. *Four golden signals*

> **Latency:** Latency is a measure of the time taken to fulfill a request.
> It is more important to critically examine the latency of failed
> requests. It is the same as duration, which we learned earlier for
> the RED method. As seen in the figure, it is advisable to track
> latency for both successful and failed requests. The average
> latency for a successful request is 134 ms, whereas that of a failed
> request is around 4 ms.

Traffic: Traffic is a measure of the requests sent to a system. In the case of a web server, this will be HTTP requests per second. In Figure 2-5, the average traffic is around 25.64 ops.

Errors: Errors are a measure of requests that fail, either explicitly (e.g., HTTP 500s) or implicitly (e.g., an HTTP 200 success response, but coupled with the wrong content). Errors can be monitored at the load balancer level for catching all HTTP 500 errors.

Saturation: A measure of the resource constraint in a system (e.g., memory in a memory-constrained system). Many systems degrade in performance with increases in utilization percentages, so having a utilization target is essential. Latency increases are often an indicator of saturation.

Types of Metrics

In the preceding sections, we learned about the different categories of metrics that one can capture and the method of measuring those metrics. In this section, we will look at the different types of metrics.

Gauges

Gauge is a point in time representation of a metric providing a single number or data point corresponding to current measurement at that time. Common metrics for utilization such as current CPU, memory, and disk usage are all represented as a gauge as the current value is of interest. Gauge, corresponding to a business metric, can be the number of users hitting HA proxy in real time or the number of items in a queue. Gauges as shown in Figure 2-6 can increase, decrease, or stay constant over time.

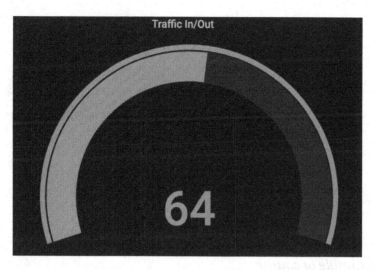

Figure 2-6. *Gauge*

Counters

Counter is another common representation, in which the number increases over time and never comes down. However, it can be reset to zero and then start incrementing again. System uptime for application or infrastructure is usually depicted as a counter. Since counters are incremental in nature, you can calculate the rate of change of a metric over a particular time period. A lot of useful information can be understood by understanding the rate of change between two values. For example, the total number of users logging in to the application is seldom useful; however, with a rate, you can check the number of logins per second, which helps in identifying the time periods of increased user activity.

Figure 2-7 shows a counter of the time-series metric of the total events watched by kube-apiserver.

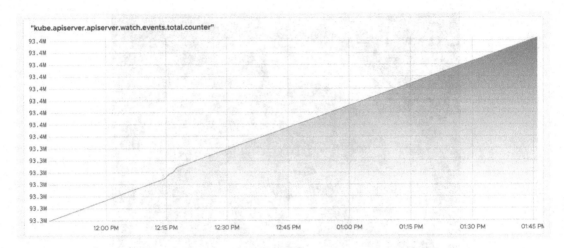

Figure 2-7. Example of counter

As seen in Figure 2-7, one can notice a fluctuation in an overall smooth ramp. Let us investigate further to ascertain what was happening during this time. Figure 2-8 shows the per second rate of change of the preceding time series, indicating that there was a spike in the number of events around 12:15 PM, thus validating our assumption.

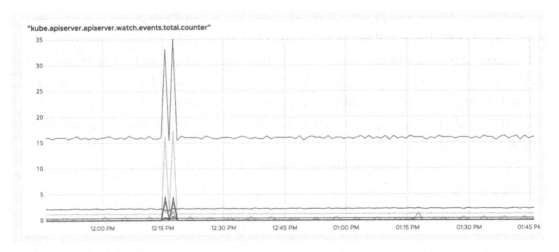

Figure 2-8. Rate of change of counter

These two figures are essential to bring to the forefront the idea that details which might not be so explicitly visible while looking at a dataset from one perspective might become interesting when looked upon from another angle. This is the remarkable capacity of metrics to tell a story hidden beneath the layers of numerical data.

Timers

Timers, as shown in Figure 2-9, represents the time taken for a request to get completed. They are used for latency measurements in application monitoring.

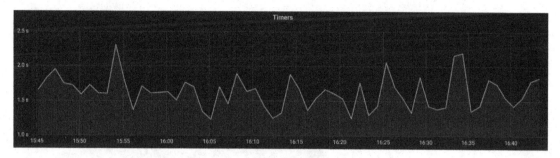

***Figure 2-9.** Example of timer*

Histograms

Containers are highly distributed and can generate an extremely large amount of monitoring metrics at high velocity. To keep up with the swarm of monitoring data, SREs use histograms and summaries. A histogram provides an approximate representation of the distribution of individual observations (usually things like request durations or response sizes) from an event or sample stream in configurable buckets. It also provides a count and sum of all observations.

A histogram with a metric name of <basemetric> would expose multiple time series during a scrape:

- cumulative counters for the observation buckets would be exposed as <basemetric>_bucket{le="<upper inclusive bound>"}

- the total sum of all observed values would be exposed as <basemetric>_sum

- the count of events that have been observed would be exposed as <basemetric>_count

Histograms as shown in the Figure 2-10, provides DevOps teams with a comprehensive view and early indication of incidents across environments while retaining granular historical visibility. Histograms can help you

- Measure and aggregate quantiles/percentiles of high-velocity metrics from multiple sources

- Measure and aggregate quantiles/percentiles of high-velocity metrics such as application response times and SLOs

When creating a histogram, it is important to consider what the buckets should be from the beginning. In most scenarios, the SLO for the metric in question can be a good place to start.

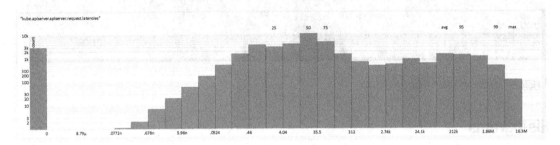

Figure 2-10. *Example of histogram*

Summary

Summary statistics as shown in Figure 2-11, provides a way to summarize a set of observations like request durations and response sizes. They can also provide total count and sum of all observations over a configurable time period. A summary with a base metric name of <basemetric> exposes multiple time series during a scrape:

- streaming **φ-quantiles** $(0 \leq \varphi \leq 1)$ of observed events, exposed as <basemetric>{quantile="<φ>"}

- the **total sum** of all observed values, exposed as <basemetric>_sum

- the **count** of events that have been observed, exposed as <basemetric>_count

Due to their simplicity and ease of calculation using just a total and a counter, averages can be used to calculate the request latency of a service; however, they have a huge drawback of hiding distribution and preventing the outliers from showing up. Quantiles are better suited to this kind of metrics, as they allow us to understand distribution. For example, if the request latency 0.95-quantile (95th percentile) is 4 s, it means that 5% of requests responded in more than 4 s.

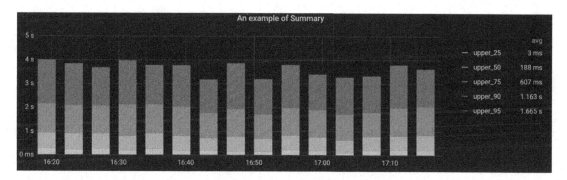

Figure 2-11. *Example of summary*

Statistical Functions

Sometimes a single metric might not be very meaningful for analysis and therefore would require mathematical transformations before we can gather meaningful details out of it. These transformations can be done on one metric or on a group of metrics. Here are some regularly used mathematical functions:

- **Count:** Count gives the number of observations for the time period under consideration.

- **Sum:** Sum returns the summation of all observations for the time period under consideration.

- **Average:** Averages are a useful metric analysis method which can help in calculating the average response time of an application. Average is a mathematical mean of all values in a specific time period.

The problem with average is that it assumes there is a normal distribution of data across the considered time period. This assumption can easily lead us to misjudgment, as lots of low values in our average would hide the few significantly high values. These hidden outliers would mean that even if we rest assured that based on the average request latency our users are experiencing a quality service, there are potentially a significant number who might not.

- **Percentile:** Percentile is a way to check the distribution of the values. For example, a 99th-percentile value of 10 milliseconds for a transaction means that 99% of transactions were completed in 10 milliseconds or less and the remaining 1% of transactions took more

than 10 milliseconds. Percentiles are ideal for identifying outliers.
If a great experience on your mobile app means a response time of
less than 10 milliseconds, then 99% of your users are having a great
experience, but 1% of them are not. You can then focus on addressing
the performance issue that's causing a problem for those 1% of users.

- **Rates of change:** Rates of change show the degree of change between
data in a time series.

Events

In addition to capturing metrics which are collected at regular intervals, it is also
important to capture events which are infrequent occurrences—such as code changes,
internal alerts, and scaling events—that can provide crucial context for understanding
the change in the behavior of a system.

Some examples of events -

- **Changes:** Internal code releases, builds, and build failures

- **Alerts:** Internally generated alerts or third-party notifications

- **Scaling events:** Adding or subtracting hosts

Since events capture the history of every individual action that happened, they
can be rolled into aggregates and can help confirm whether or not a particular action
occurred at the given time. For this reason, engineers may want to collect every event
that happens all the time, which is not feasible, as every event takes some compute and
storage space to collect and that's costly. So, it makes sense to capture events which are
infrequent but critical in nature. In case one wants to collect continuously a given event
with context, then you should consider capturing metrics instead.

For example:

Event	Timestamp	Additional attribute
Hotfix no. ### released to production	2020–05–15 04:13:25 UTC	Time elapsed: 2.8 seconds
Pull request ## merged	2020–05–19 14:22:20 UTC	Commits: io911e7
Nightly backup failed	2020–05–27 00:01:18 UTC	Link to logs of failed backup

Events are also used to generate alerts, as some of these can be extremely rare but critical events that would require some intervention from an operator; for example, failure of the nightly backup. However, more often events are only used to investigate the occurrence of a particular event and correlate issues that may have occurred across systems.

An event log is an immutable, timestamped record of discrete events that happened over time. Each event entry is classified by type to identify the severity of the event. These are mentioned in the following:

Event Type	Description
Information	An event that describes the successful operation of a task, such as an application, driver, or service.
Warning	An event that describes the successful operation of a task but in a way that is not recommended.
Error	An event that is not necessarily significant but may indicate the possible occurrence of a future problem.
Success Audit (Security log)	An event that describes the successful completion of an audited security event.
Failure Audit (Security log)	An event that describes an audited security event that did not complete successfully.

Observability of Kubernetes

Traditionally, companies used to monitor only two stacks: applications and the infrastructure running them. With the advent of containers and then Kubernetes, there are now other components that need to be monitored as well. Monitoring Kubernetes helps in identification of whether a Kubernetes environment—clusters, nodes, pods, containers, and application workloads—are operating as per expectation. Prometheus is the most popular open source solution for monitoring Kubernetes and provides real-time monitoring, alerting, and time-series database functionalities for modern cloud native applications as depicted in Figure 2-12. It is a simple yet powerful monitoring tool that can help you identify symptoms and rectify if anything is wrong. We will learn about Prometheus in more detail in Part 2 of this book.

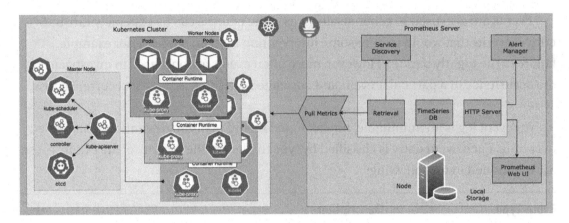

Figure 2-12. *Observability of Kubernetes using Prometheus*

Monitoring is great but in order to better understand how workloads running on Kubernetes influence the performance of applications and rectify problems before they can become end-user problems, we need to extend the same concepts we learned earlier in observability to Kubernetes. Kubernetes observability provides developers with a complete picture necessary for improving performance and increasing the stability and resiliency of applications, the Kubernetes components themselves, and the underlying infrastructure. Observability tools for Kubernetes include comprehensive overviews, intelligent summaries and alerts, and ways to correlate metrics coming from all these different stacks.

Observability is crucial in a dynamic environment to understand the interactions between the application services and the Kubernetes infrastructure they are running on. Data from Kubernetes clusters needs to be correlated with application data to isolate particular service-facing problems. Sometimes Kubernetes will manage the clusters so well that it would be difficult to become aware of a problem with the infrastructure. For example, Kubernetes might restart your application, and you would never notice that your containers crashed multiple times due to memory leaks. This can lead to grave problems at a later stage if neglected for long. A robust mechanism that can inform about saturation, throughput, and errors in the Kubernetes pods and the corresponding application services helps in alerting about any anomalous behavior.

Sources of Metrics in Kubernetes

Kubernetes components, both master node and worker nodes, generate a lot of metrics and that too in Prometheus format. These metrics can help us understand the inner workings of the Kubernetes system as well as the impact on applications. The output in Prometheus format is structured plain text which can be read by humans or used as an input to other monitoring engines. There are various internal sources like Container Advisor (cAdvisor), Kubernetes API Server, and Metrics Server which can fetch system-level metrics. There are sources like kube-state-metrics and Prometheus Node Exporter which can fetch application-level metrics as well. In this section, we will look at the metrics sources and an overview of metrics they produce.

The following steps assume that a Kubernetes cluster has already been set up. Readers are advised to use Minikube or Kind to setup a Kubernetes cluster by following instructions available at `https://kubernetes.io/docs/tasks/tools/`. Once the Kubernetes cluster is up and running and kubectl has been installed successfully, the first thing to do is to list all the pods in the cluster using the following command:

```
$ kubectl get pods –all-namespaces
```

This command should produce an output similar to the one in Figure 2-13. The important component to look out for is the **kube-apiserver** (or kube-apiserver-minikube in case you used Minikube to set up the cluster), which should be up and running.

```
[mainakc@147dda0fdf56 ~ % kubectl get pods --all-namespaces
NAMESPACE              NAME                                        READY   STATUS    RESTARTS   AGE
kube-system            coredns-66bff467f8-n9jvm                    1/1     Running   0          8m26s
kube-system            etcd-minikube                               1/1     Running   0          8m8s
kube-system            kube-apiserver-minikube                     1/1     Running   2          8m53s
kube-system            kube-controller-manager-minikube            1/1     Running   4          8m53s
kube-system            kube-proxy-ghsd6                            1/1     Running   0          8m26s
kube-system            kube-scheduler-minikube                     1/1     Running   1          7m49s
kube-system            storage-provisioner                         1/1     Running   0          8m32s
kubernetes-dashboard   dashboard-metrics-scraper-dc6947fbf-g74dd   1/1     Running   0          8m26s
kubernetes-dashboard   kubernetes-dashboard-6dbb54fd95-xcthl       1/1     Running   0          8m26s
[mainakc@147dda0fdf56 ~ % kubectl proxy
Starting to serve on 127.0.0.1:8001
```

Figure 2-13. *List of pods*

Kubernetes API Server

kube-apiserver is the central management plane of Kubernetes that communicates with the entire cluster. All the user requests pass through the API Server after client request validation, and it interacts with etcd for persistence of cluster state. Kube-apiserver serves the Kubernetes API, which is used internally by the worker nodes for communication as well as externally by kubectl.

It provides a number of critical metrics—the request rate, error rate, and duration (RED metrics)—for Kubernetes resources. It also emits data related to count, health, and availability of pods, nodes, and other Kubernetes objects. In order to view this information, we need to proxy the request between our local machine and the kube-apiserver. To start a proxy server in the background, use the following command:

```
$ kubectl proxy
```

This should start a proxy, and you can view all the metrics from the kube-apiserver at `http://localhost:8001/metrics` as displayed in Figure 2-14:

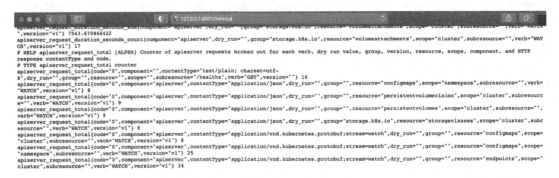

Figure 2-14. *Metrics from kube-apiserver*

The metrics are in a Prometheus text format and preceded by # HELP and # TYPE to explain the metric and the associated format for readability. Some of the other metrics captured from the kube-apiservers are shown in Figure 2-15.

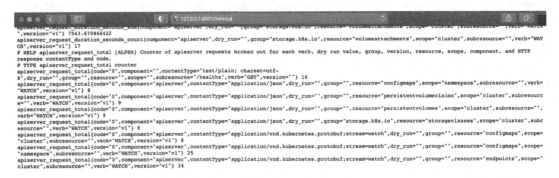

Figure 2-15. *More metrics from the kube-apiserver*

cAdvisor

cAdvisor is a container analysis tool that collects, aggregates, and exports performance and usage metrics about all running containers. It provides quick information about CPU, memory, and network usage statistics of running containers. cAdvisor is embedded into the kubelet, hence you can scrape the kubelet to get container metrics. It tracks and retains telemetry for each running container including historical resource utilization, distributions (histogram metrics) of complete historical resource utilization, network metrics, resource isolation parameters, and many more. It can provide basic machine-level performance characteristics but lacks analytics and persistence to understand trends.

To access the cAdvisor metrics, we need to proxy between our machine and the Kubernetes API Server. Start a local instance of the proxy server by typing the following:

```
$ kubectl proxy
```

This should start a proxy, and you can view all the metrics at `http://localhost:8001/api/v1/nodes/minikube/proxy/metrics/cadvisor` as shown in Figure 2-16:

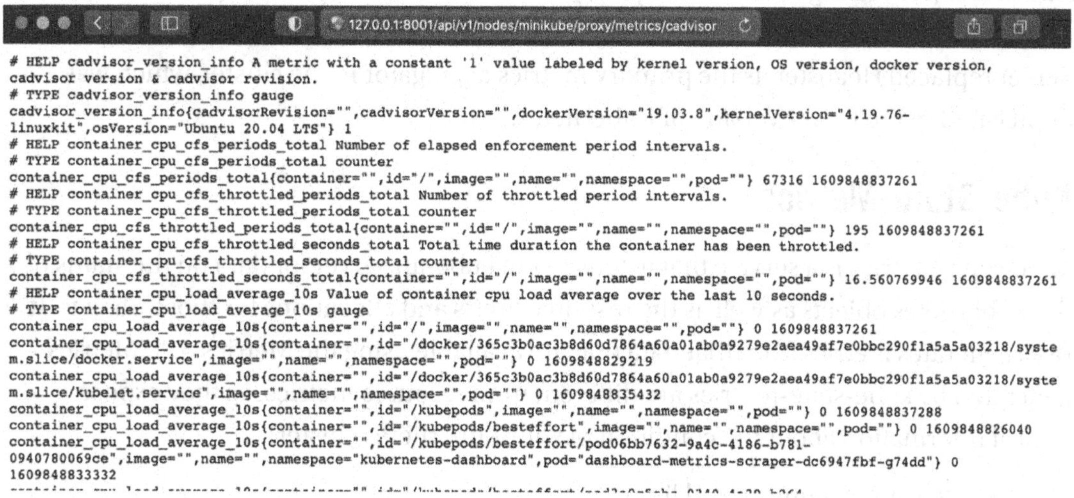


```
# HELP cadvisor_version_info A metric with a constant '1' value labeled by kernel version, OS version, docker version,
cadvisor version & cadvisor revision.
# TYPE cadvisor_version_info gauge
cadvisor_version_info{cadvisorRevision="",cadvisorVersion="",dockerVersion="19.03.8",kernelVersion="4.19.76-
linuxkit",osVersion="Ubuntu 20.04 LTS"} 1
# HELP container_cpu_cfs_periods_total Number of elapsed enforcement period intervals.
# TYPE container_cpu_cfs_periods_total counter
container_cpu_cfs_periods_total{container="",id="/",image="",name="",namespace="",pod=""} 67316 1609848837261
# HELP container_cpu_cfs_throttled_periods_total Number of throttled period intervals.
# TYPE container_cpu_cfs_throttled_periods_total counter
container_cpu_cfs_throttled_periods_total{container="",id="/",image="",name="",namespace="",pod=""} 195 1609848837261
# HELP container_cpu_cfs_throttled_seconds_total Total time duration the container has been throttled.
# TYPE container_cpu_cfs_throttled_seconds_total counter
container_cpu_cfs_throttled_seconds_total{container="",id="/",image="",name="",namespace="",pod=""} 16.560769946 1609848837261
# HELP container_cpu_load_average_10s Value of container cpu load average over the last 10 seconds.
# TYPE container_cpu_load_average_10s gauge
container_cpu_load_average_10s{container="",id="/",image="",name="",namespace="",pod=""} 0 1609848837261
container_cpu_load_average_10s{container="",id="/docker/365c3b0ac3b8d60d7864a60a01ab0a9279e2aea49af7e0bbc290f1a5a5a03218/syste
m.slice/docker.service",image="",name="",namespace="",pod=""} 0 1609848829219
container_cpu_load_average_10s{container="",id="/docker/365c3b0ac3b8d60d7864a60a01ab0a9279e2aea49af7e0bbc290f1a5a5a03218/syste
m.slice/kubelet.service",image="",name="",namespace="",pod=""} 0 1609848835432
container_cpu_load_average_10s{container="",id="/kubepods",image="",name="",namespace="",pod=""} 0 1609848837288
container_cpu_load_average_10s{container="",id="/kubepods/besteffort",image="",name="",namespace="",pod=""} 0 1609848826040
container_cpu_load_average_10s{container="",id="/kubepods/besteffort/pod06bb7632-9a4c-4186-b781-
0940780069ce",image="",name="",namespace="kubernetes-dashboard",pod="dashboard-metrics-scraper-dc6947fbf-g74dd"} 0
1609848833332
```

Figure 2-16. *cAdvisor metrics*

When these metrics from cAdvisor are sent to a visualization back end, we can get such insightful charts as shown in Figure 2-17, which shows the CPU usage percentage of a docker container.

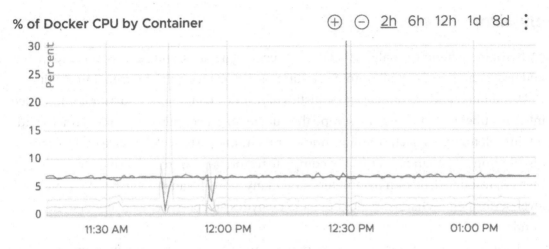

Figure 2-17. *Metrics from cAdvisor*

Kubernetes Metrics Server

Kubernetes Metrics Server is a source of container resource metrics like CPU and memory usage of the Kubernetes cluster. It collects these metrics from kubelets and exposes them in kube-apiserver through Metrics API for use by Horizontal Pod Autoscaler (for scaling up container pods) and Vertical Pod Autoscaler (for automatically adjusting resources). Metrics Server is not meant for non-autoscaling purposes. Metrics Server replaced Heapster as the primary metrics aggregator in the cluster, which was deprecated in the newer version of Kubernetes.

Kube-State-Metrics

kube-state-metrics is a service that listens to the kube-apiserver for data on the status of the Kubernetes objects as well as the resource limits and allocations for those objects. It then generates metrics from that data that are available using the Metrics API. Metrics generated by kube-state-metrics are different from resource metrics, as they expose critical information about the condition of your Kubernetes cluster:

- Resource requests and limits

- Number of pods in a running/terminated/failed state

- Number of objects: nodes, pods, services, deployments

Kubernetes Internal Metrics

The master nodes are responsible for running the Kubernetes control plane, which in turn monitors the cluster, makes scheduling decisions, and ensures that the cluster runs in its desired state. Hence, it's critical to collect key metrics and monitor the control plane components, like API Server, scheduler, controller, and etcd, and visualize them in one place. These metrics provide a detailed view of the cluster performance and also assist in troubleshooting issues. Since all the components are running as containers, let us first see the most important container metrics:

Container Metrics		Description
Summary Usage	Containers running	Total number of containers running
	Host CPU usage	CPU usage of the host on which container runs
	Host storage usage	Storage usage of the host on which container runs
	Host memory usage	Memory usage of the host on which container runs
CPU	CPU usage by container	CPU usage of the container under observation
	Total container and system CPU usage	CPU usage of the container and the system
Memory	Memory usage by container in bytes	Memory usage of the container under observation measured in bytes
	Memory usage %	Memory usage % of the container under observation
Networking	Bytes received by container	Bytes received over the network by the container
	Bytes transferred by container	Bytes transmitted over the network by the container
	Networking errors by container	Network errors, connection resets by container
Storage	Total disk usage	Disk usage by the container
	Disk I/O	Disk IOPS by the container

Kubernetes Metrics		Description
Summary Usage	Nodes	Total no. of nodes in a Kubernetes cluster
	Pods	Total no. of pods in a Kubernetes cluster
	Pod containers	Total no. of pod containers in a Kubernetes cluster
	Namespaces	Total no. of namespaces in a Kubernetes cluster
	Average node CPU utilization	Average CPU utilization % by node
	Average node memory utilization	Average memory utilization % by node
	Average node storage utilization	Average storage utilization % by node
	Cluster memory usage	Memory usage of the Kubernetes cluster
Namespaces	Pod count by namespaces	Total no. of pods in a namespace
	Pod container count by namespaces	Total no. of pod containers in a namespace
	Memory usage by namespaces	Total memory usage in a namespace
Node	CPU utilization by node	CPU utilization % of a node
	CPU usage by node	CPU usage by a node
	Memory utilization by node	Memory utilization % of a node
	Memory usage by node	Memory usage by a node
	Bytes received rate by node	Rate of bytes received over the network by the node
	Bytes transferred rate by node	Rate of bytes transferred over the network by the node
	File system usage %	File system usage % by node
	File system usage by node	File system used by node in bytes
	File system available storage by node	File system available in node in bytes

(*continued*)

Kubernetes Metrics		Description
Pod	CPU usage rate by pod	CPU utilization % of a pod
	Memory usage by pod	Memory usage by a pod
	Bytes received rate by pod	Rate of bytes received over the network by the node
	Bytes transferred rate by pod	Rate of bytes transferred over the network by the node
	File system usage by pod	File system usage % by node

Operations in a Kubernetes Environment

Since Kubernetes doesn't optimize performance directly by itself, developers have to identify and tune individual resources across the stack like hosts, clusters, containers, and applications. Every container and pod is different; some might be CPU hungry, whereas others might be running I/O-intensive workloads. To understand performance parameters in a Kubernetes environment, operators must ask these questions:

- What are the utilization levels across CPU and memory? Is there any node which is facing resource contention?

- What is the latency experienced by the pods? Do some pods face more latency than others in a cluster?

- Why is there a performance hit when autoscaling was initiated? Is autoscaling responsible for performance lag? Are there performance hits from multi-tenancy?

- Do underlying dependencies hamper performance of the applications?

It is the overall responsibility of both development and SRE teams to look into the performance of the application and ensure that overall SLOs are met:

- Developers define SLOs using metrics such as page load times, caching behavior, and transaction times for improving software quality.

- SREs take care of platform services that are critical dependencies to applications and services. They use SLOs to support the quality of high-velocity software release life cycles.

Decisions are made based on correlating the SLOs of developers and SREs with that of the business. After a change is made to the environment, developers and SREs correlate the application data and the data from the Kubernetes control plane to understand the impact of those changes on the overall environment. This process reveals the dependencies between the Kubernetes components and the workloads they run.

For example, if some of the pods in the Kubernetes clusters are overloaded or misconfigured, all other operations within the cluster and the deployed application may get impacted as well. While SREs and platform engineers need to operate the Kubernetes orchestration layer, developers must understand the impact of the Kubernetes orchestration layer on their applications and microservices. Therefore, their challenges are different, as listed in the following table.

Developers' Challenges	SREs' Challenges
• Resolve mismatch between desired and actual state (applications/workloads, container images, number of replicas, network and disk resources) for better resource usage and application performance	• Ensure that the Kubernetes components operate as expected (e.g., over- or underallocated resources may cause nonstarting or crashing pods under high workloads)
• Operate workloads within specified resource limits for their applications or microservices (e.g., increased number of pods per node can lead to service latencies)	• Run within cloud provider limits (e.g., if a container exceeds its memory limit, Kubernetes might terminate it)
• Take care of upstream and downstream dependencies	• Understand etcd load per object because major etcd failure will cripple or take down the container infrastructure
• Prevent pod failures	• Avoid node hotspots (e.g., nodes with low memory or disk capacity)

Though their challenges are different, both developers and SREs would need to ingest, observe, be alert about, and understand the data flow and the metrics exposed through Kubernetes. They also need to collaborate together to effectively run the containerized application on the Kubernetes platform.

CHAPTER 3

Architecture of a Modern Monitoring System

In the first chapter of this book, we learned about monitoring and cloud native concepts, focusing on the essential terminologies and ideas that are foundational to the design of monitoring systems. In the second chapter we discussed observability and why is it so important for understanding the dynamics of a microservices-based modern application. We took a look at the pillars of observability—metrics, logs, and traces— and then explored the possibilities of observing a Kubernetes environment through the same lens. By now we have established the reasons behind the need for an end-to-end observability solution, which I would colloquially refer to as a modern monitoring system, for cloud native applications.

In this chapter, we will look at the individual components of monitoring, understanding their functions and how they fit into the overall modern monitoring system. We will design an end-to-end architecture that is capable of identification of the minutest problems affecting your systems and then alerting you in the shortest possible time. By the end of this chapter, and also the end of Part 1 of this book, the reader will have a solid understanding of monitoring in general, its components and frameworks, the design of what a monitoring system should include, and the associated terms and concepts.

Before we get down to design that architecture, we need to first identify the individual components that will make up this monitoring platform. These individual components are

- Data collection

- Data storage

- Data analysis/query engine

- Data visualization

© Mainak Chakraborty and Ajit Pratap Kundan 2021
M. Chakraborty and A. P. Kundan, *Monitoring Cloud-Native Applications*,
https://doi.org/10.1007/978-1-4842-6888-9_3

- Alerting engine

- Log aggregation

- Distributed tracing

The life cycle of monitoring data passes through each of these components before being eventually discarded due to staleness. Output from the data analysis stage acts as an input to the data lake for business intelligence (BI) and analytics systems and therefore survives in a different form. Some industries are regulated to store logs for an extended time period; therefore, those are persisted on either long-term archival solutions or moved offsite on tape.

Modern Monitoring System Architecture

A modern monitoring system consists broadly of the seven components enumerated previously. Some of the commercially available monitoring tools cater to some or all of these areas, but are generally more suited to solving one particular problem very well, rather than solving all of them. The same observation holds true for open source tools as well. Therefore, you will often find enterprises opting for more than one tool while deciding their observability strategy.

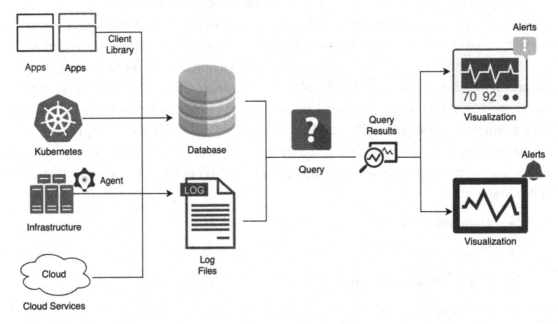

Figure 3-1. *Architecture of a modern monitoring system*

As seen in Figure 3-1, telemetry data can be collected from applications (through client library instrumentation), Kubernetes clusters, infrastructure systems (through agent deployments) and cloud services. In some scenarios, cloud services can also host underlying infrastructure and run Kubernetes as a managed offering. Telemetry data thus collected can be stored in a database (time-series database [TSDB]). Using a query engine, one can run queries on the stored data or the log files generated from the preceding input sources. The queried results can then be easily sent to one or more visualization back ends. These visualization platforms are capable of transforming the machine-generated data into meaningful charts and graphs. Operations teams can infer this data to understand the internal workings of the complete environment and compare it against desired outputs. They can also create actionable alerts which will trigger in case of any unexpected behavioral pattern. Once an alert is triggered, a preallotted operations team member can be notified to resolve the problem or else automation scripts can be executed to rectify the issue without any manual intervention. Also, distributed tracing can help in identifying the areas causing performance issues or latency in service to in services communication. This is the modern-day monitoring system architecture that we are going to learn about in this chapter.

Data Collection

There are generally two ways to collect data from your infrastructure, applications, or cloud environment. You can either use an agent or a collector or instrument your application to send telemetry data. However, these systems have their own proprietary formats in which they generate this data which may or may not be understood by your monitoring system of choice. In order to solve this issue, we will generate data in one of the data formats compatible with the monitoring back end by using one of the approaches mentioned in the following:

Instrumenting Your Code

You can use the client libraries, specific to the language in which your application is written, to instrument your application code. This will define and expose the internal application metrics on your application's instance via an HTTP endpoint.

For example, in the case of Prometheus, you can choose from the official client libraries available in Go, Java, Ruby, and Python or any one of the unofficially available third-party client libraries to instrument your code. Let us look at an example of the Go client library, which can be used to expose Prometheus metrics from a Go application.

Firstly, we need to install the Golang client libraries using the go get command:

```
$ go get github.com/prometheus/client_golang/prometheus
$ go get github.com/prometheus/client_golang/prometheus/promauto
$ go get github.com/prometheus/client_golang/prometheus/promhttp
```

You can expose the Prometheus metrics from the application by providing a "/metrics" HTTP endpoint using the HTTP handler function from the promhttp library installed previously.

```
1    package main
2
3    import (
4            "net/http"
5            "github.com/prometheus/client_golang/prometheus/promhttp"
6    )
7
8    func main() {
9            http.Handle("/metrics", promhttp.Handler())
10           http.ListenAndServe(":8080", nil)
11   }
```

Figure 3-2. *Exposing metrics from a Go application*

The application will now start exposing the default Go metrics at Port 8080. We can configure a Prometheus instance to scrape the incoming metrics to make them visible in Prometheus UI or one can directly check them at http://localhost:8080/metrics.

The example in Figure 3-2 shows a very simple mechanism to expose the default Go metrics; however, in case you want to add custom metrics in order to expose the application specific metrics, you can follow the following example:

```
1    package main
2
3    import (
4            "net/http"
5            "time"
6            "github.com/prometheus/client_golang/prometheus"
7            "github.com/prometheus/client_golang/prometheus/promauto"
8            "github.com/prometheus/client_golang/prometheus/promhttp"
9    )
10
11   func recordMetrics() {
12           go func() {
13                   for {
14                           opsProcessed.Inc()
15                           time.Sleep(5 * time.Second)
16                   }
17           }()
18   }
19
20   var (
21           opsProcessed = promauto.NewCounter(prometheus.CounterOpts{
22                   Name: "total_processed_ops",
23                   Help: "The total number of operations processed",
24           })
25   )
26
27   func main() {
28           recordMetrics()
29
30           http.Handle("/metrics", promhttp.Handler())
31           http.ListenAndServe(":8080", nil)
32   }
```

Figure 3-3. *Adding custom metrics to an application*

In the example in Figure 3-3, we are first importing the client library modules and then defining a counter metric called opsProcessed, which will inform us about the total number of operations processed till then. The Inc() method increases the counter values by 1. We are using promauto in this example, which will automatically register the new metric with the default registry.

When you run the new program, this application-specific metric, opsProcessed, will appear under /metrics. You can use the Prometheus query language, PromQL, to query using an expression like *rate(opsProcessed[1m]*, which will show the rate of change of the previous metric over time. We will learn more about Prometheus and PromQL in Chapter 4.

Exposition

Exposition refers to the process of exposing the collected metrics over HTTP at the /
metrics path. Instrumenting the code will only generate the metrics, but these metrics
have to be sent to the monitoring system, and exposition is the process which takes care
of that. The exposition request is handled by the client library and is included either in
the main function or another top-level function.

By default, metrics are served at /metrics but it can be configured on other paths as
well if /metrics is already in use. If the path is configured to something else, the endpoint
is still commonly referred to as /metrics only. After the metrics are defined, they are
usually registered with the default registry. If you are using a client library which has
Prometheus instrumentation, the metrics will be in the default registry without the need
for any additional instrumentation explicitly.

Metrics exposed for processing with Prometheus are in a text-based format, which
is easy to understand as it is human-readable and therefore easy to assemble. The
limitations are that it can be verbose and have a cost of parsing attached to it. The text-
based format of Prometheus is line oriented, and a line feed character (\n) is used to
separate the lines. The last line must end with a line feed character.

The Prometheus text-based format is shown in the following:

```
metric_name [
  "{" label_name "=" `"` label_value `"` { "," label_name "=" `"`
  label_value `"` } [ "," ] "}"
] value [ timestamp ]
```

InfluxDB uses a line protocol to write data points in a text-based format that provides
the measurement, tag set, field set, and timestamp of a data point. The InfluxDB text
format is shown in the following:

```
<measurement>[,<tag_key>=<tag_value>[,<tag_key>=<tag_value>]]
<field_key>=<field_value>[,<field_key>=<field_value>] [<timestamp>]
// Example
myMeasurement,tag1=value1,tag2=value2 fieldKey="fieldValue"
1556813561098000000

// Example
myMeasurement,tag1=value1,tag2=value2 fieldKey="fieldValue"
1556813561098000000
```

Bridges

Client libraries of Prometheus don't output metrics just in Prometheus Text format. In case you want to instrument using Prometheus but expose the metrics to another output like Graphite or Grafana back end, you can use bridges. A bridge takes output of the metrics from the client library registry and sends it to other monitoring systems. The client libraries for Python, Java, and Go include a Graphite bridge which can convert the metrics into a format which is understood by Graphite and writes them out to it.

Parsers

Client libraries for Python and Go clients also feature a parser for the Prometheus exposition format. Other monitoring systems like InfluxDB, DataDog, and Sensu can parse the Prometheus text format, so you can instrument your application for exposing Prometheus metrics and send the output to any of the other systems directly and never even run Prometheus server.

Third-Party Exporters

In those scenarios, where it is not feasible to instrument third-party applications or systems which you are using, third-party exporters are available to export existing metrics in Prometheus. In the case of InfluxDB, you can configure third-party technologies like Apache, JMeter, and FluentD to send line protocol directly to InfluxDB.

Agents

Agents are used to directly collect metrics from the systems on which they are installed or pull metrics from third-party APIs without any or very minimal code instrumentation. In this section, we take a look at a couple of open source metric collection agents/tools:

collectd

It is a popular open source systems statistics collection daemon which can gather metrics from many sources like applications, operating systems, external hardware devices, and logfiles. It then makes this information available over the network. collectd is written in C for better performance and easy portability. It comes with support for more than 100 plug-ins and can run on systems without the need for any special scripting. While collectd can collect a lot of metrics, it can't generate graphs and its monitoring functionality is also limited to basic threshold checking.

StatsD

It is an open source network daemon that listens for statistics like counter and timers and sends aggregated stats to one or more supported back-end services like Graphite, DataDog, Elasticsearch, InfluxDB, and so on. It is written in Node.js and optimized toward counting events and submitting aggregated counts.

StatsD is popular for its ability to collect data very quickly. The StatsD client collects data and sends it quickly using UDP assuming that it will reach the StatsD daemon and doesn't wait for a handshake. The StatsD daemon listens for UDP traffic coming from the client. The daemon collects data, aggregates it, and sends it to a back-end system every 10 seconds by default, effectively making it near real time.

Telegraf

It is part of the TICK[1] stack (now InfluxDB OSS 2.0) and available as a stand-alone open source plug-in-based agent that collects, processes, aggregates, and writes metrics. It can collect metrics from applications, systems, networking devices, databases, message queues, and even IoT sensors. It is written in Go, which means that it compiles into a single binary which can be executed on any system without any external dependencies.

Telegraf supports over 200+ plug-ins out of the box. Telegraf plug-ins support parsers (input data formats) and serializers (output data formats), which can be added to Telegraf plug-ins that include the data format option.

fluentd

It is an open source data collector that lets you unify the log data collection from multiple sources for better correlation and understanding. It was the sixth project to graduate from CNCF after immensely successful projects like Kubernetes, Prometheus, Envoy, CoreDNS, and containerd. Fluentd solves the problems related to logging at scale, not just for regular stand-alone applications but also for the distributed architecture of cloud native applications, making it an integral tool for any cloud native organization.

---

[1]Telegraf, InfluxDB, Chronograf, and Kapacitor (TICK) Stack

fluentd collects logs from various data sources and tries to structure it as JSON, which allows it to create what is called the **unified logging layer** by combining all facets of log data processing—collecting, filtering, buffering, and sending logs. fluentd is written in a combination of C and Ruby. The fluentd instance has a memory footprint of 30-40MB and can process 13,000 events/second/core.

Now, since we have seen the process of data collection from disparate systems and applications, let's take a closer look at the OpenTelemetry project and examine how it aims to solve the major issues surrounding data collection from proprietary sources. OpenTelemetry aims to radically simplify the process of data collection by defining standard API and tooling which can be combined with existing systems to generate output in open source observability data formats (Prometheus, Jaeger, etc.).

OpenTelemetry

Distributed architectures are inherently more complex and introduce a wide variety of operational challenges with regards to performance and availability. In order to solve this problem, we need telemetry data which can help us observe these environments better. Now telemetry data is provided mostly by commercial vendors for their own solutions. Since there is no standardization in the format of telemetry data collected, there can be no data portability between back ends. Organizations have to maintain their own sets of instrumentation to achieve data compatibility. OpenTelemetry tries to solve this challenge by introducing a vendor-neutral solution with broad support from cloud providers, vendors, and enterprises.

OpenTelemetry is a framework for observability that provides the power to capture telemetry data from multiple input sources using a set of predefined libraries, agents, and tools so that you can better observe and manage them. In other words, OpenTelemetry can capture metrics, logs, resource metadata, and distributed traces from your applications and send them to a compatible back end such as Prometheus, Jaeger, orand Zipkin for processing. The official definition of OpenTelemetry as per the OpenTelemetry project is as follows:

OpenTelemetry is a set of APIs, SDKs, tooling and integrations that are designed for the creation and management of telemetry data such as traces, metrics, and logs.

OpenTelemetry is important because it provides

- Vendor-agnostic APIs and SDK with support for automatic and manual instrumentation

- Ability to generate, collect, process, and export telemetry data to multiple destinations in parallel with support for managing samples and context propagation

- Agents that can collect telemetry from some applications without requiring code changes

- Support for a variety of open source and commercial protocols, format and context propagation mechanisms, as well as providing shims to the OpenTracing and OpenCensus projects

OpenTelemetry is a sandbox project of CNCF, formed as a result of the merger of OpenTracing[2] and OpenCensus[3] projects. It aims to define and standardize the way in which telemetry data is received, processed, and stored from different sources. OpenTelemetry eliminates the need to run, operate, and maintain several open source or proprietary agents and collectors in order to run your monitoring systems successfully, whether they be open source tools or commercial offerings.

There are two ways of exporting telemetry data using OpenTelemetry. The first one is to directly export it from the process using OpenTelemetry APIs and SDKs. After configuring the API and the SDK, you can create metrics and traces either by using meter and tracer objects from the provider or by utilizing a plug-in to create those for you. This mechanism requires you to use one or more libraries to translate the in-memory spans and metrices into a suitable format which can be sent over to an analysis back end like Prometheus or Jaeger.

The other mechanism uses OpenTelemetry Protocol (OTLP), a wire protocol, to send data to the OpenTelemetry collector. The collector is a standard binary process that can be run as a proxy or a sidecar along with the instances or it can also be run separately on a different host. The collector can be configured to forward the data it is collecting to any supported analysis back ends. There are several open source and commercial tools that support OpenTelemetry data for analysis.

---

[2]opentracing.io
[3]opencensus.io

OpenTelemetry Collector

OpenTelemetry collector allows you to receive telemetry data from various sources without running multiple agents. It just doesn't receive but also optionally transforms and sends the data further in the default configuration itself and without the need to make any specific changes to the core code. It has a single unified code base that supports metrics, logs, and traces.

As defined by the project community:

> *The OpenTelemetry Collector offers a vendor-agnostic implementation on how to receive, process, and export telemetry data. In addition, it removes the need to run, operate, and maintain multiple agents/collectors in order to support open source telemetry data formats (e.g., Jaeger, Prometheus, etc.) sending to multiple open source or commercial back ends.*

OpenTelemetry Collector Architecture

OpenTelemetry collector supports several protocols (open source) for receiving telemetry data, transforming it, and then sending it further to other back-end systems. The collector is an executable and offers a pluggable architecture for adding more protocols to it as seen in Figure 3-4:

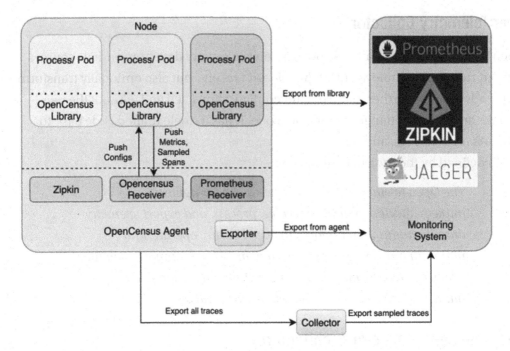

Figure 3-4. *OpenTelemetry architecture*

Agent

An agent can be deployed as a binary, as a daemonset, or as a sidecar to be run along with the application. It is generally deployed on all the hosts in the environment and is capable of adding rich metadata to the telemetry data so that you can slice and dice data as per the query needed. The activities for batching, encryption, compression, and so forth can be offloaded to the agent, thus saving the effort for individual client instrumentation for these activities.

Gateway

The second deployment method is that of a gateway which can be deployed in either the cluster or the datacenter. It runs as a stand-alone service and offers advanced capabilities such as tail-based sampling over the agent. Since it is deployed as a single component, it limits the number of points where data needs to be sent. In case the architecture needs to be scaled up, it can be easily done as all of the collectors operate independently from each other.

Open Telemetry Agent

OpenTelemetry library records, collects, samples, and aggregates on metrics and spans from applications running in pods or a VM and exports the collected data to persistent storage back end using library exporters. This is a complex process, as each time the exporter has to be implemented in the language of the application, and if using Ruby or PHP, it is difficult to do statistical aggregation. Another option is to run the OpenTelemetry collector as an agent which can be deployed independent of the library. The agent runs as a daemon and can retrieve metrics and spans from the library and then send them to other back ends. Agent can also do the aggregation on raw measurements if the native language doesn't support statistical aggregation.

Data Storage

Storing the telemetry data is an important component of any robust monitoring system architecture. There are two schools of thought on this subject, with most favoring the NoSQL model for storing the data and with some still standing by the relational database model. The reason for adopting a NoSQL database is that time-series data tend to increase with time, becoming ill-suited for a relational database. In a relational database, a table is stored as a set of fixed-size pages (8KB in PostgreSQL), on which the system then adds data structures (B-Trees) to index this data. Using the index, it becomes quicker for a query to find a row having the specific data without scanning the entire table. This works smoothly as long as the dataset and indexes are small and can be accommodated in memory. However, if the dataset is so large that it can't be stored in memory, then it has to be stored in disk, and updating a random part would mean significant disk I/O as we go back and forth reading pages from disk into memory, modifying it in memory, and then writing back to the disk. Since the database will access only a page from the disk at a time, even small updates can mean a lot of swaps which can ultimately be time consuming. We would look at how this issue is solved through NoSQL.

In this section, we will learn in detail about the specific implementation of the NoSQL data model as TSDB, designed to store timestamped observability data. We will also look at the Log-Structured-Merge-Tree (LSM-Tree) storage engine and why many open source systems use it as the underlying platform for storage.

LSM-Tree

LSM-Trees are used by a wide range of NoSQL databases to reduce the cost of making small writes by performing large append-only writes to disk. It doesn't do "in-place" writes, as doing a small change to an existing page would mean reading the entire page from disk to memory and then writing it back to disk. So, LSM-Tree queues up several updates into pages and then writes them as a single batch to disk. All writes are performed to a sorted table stored in memory, and then flushed to disk as one single immutable batch in Sorted String Table (SSTable) when it grows to a sufficient size.

In LSM-Tree implementation as an SSTable, data is a stored as a key/value pair. The index file stores changes made in a certain duration as batches. LSM-Tree then utilizes this information from the index files to merge-sort for each fragment of data file and cache in the memory. This provides low latency for data retrieval. Since the cache is immutable, new records will be inserted into new files. From time to time, files are merged together to keep to a small number of files at any given point of time. In Figure 3-5, a generic representation of LSM-Tree is shown.

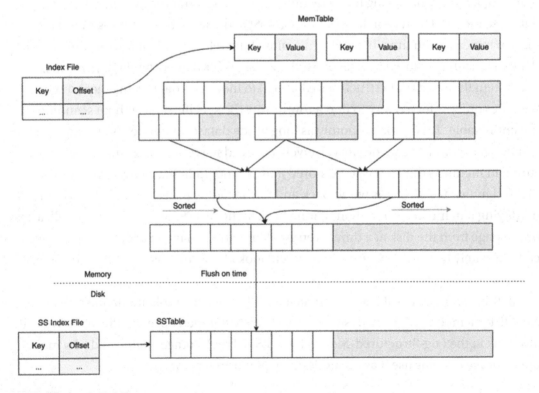

Figure 3-5. *LSM-Tree*

Now this takes care of the writes; however, any indexed search requiring fast response will have low I/O efficiency. Therefore, the LSM-Tree might be most suited for inserts than data retrievals. The common method to make the reads faster is to hold a page-index in-memory. Since the data is index sorted, the search can look up directly for the target key. This process would introduce other tradeoffs like higher memory requirements and poor secondary index support, which we look at in detail in the following:

- **Higher memory requirements:** In an LSM-Tree there is no global index and no single ordering to give a sorted order over all keys. So, the entire process of searching for a value gets more difficult, as first it checks the memory table for the latest version of the key and if it is not present then looks at many on-disk tables to find the latest value associated with that key. This can result in excessive disk I/O; therefore, to avoid this problem, all SSTables are kept in memory entirely, thus increasing the memory requirements.

- **Secondary index support:** Since LSM-Trees don't have any global sorting order, they don't support secondary indexes. Some systems either duplicate the data in a different order or build their primary keys as a combination of multiple key values. This process adds to a large scan for keys at the time of the query. Therefore, the LSM-Tree supports items with limited cardinality.[4]

Time-Series Data

Time-series data is a collection of observations for a specific measurement over a particular time range. Measurement of temperature at a particular location over a period of 5 days can be represented as time series. Figure 3-6 showing the movement of NASDAQ over a 1-day period is also time-series data, as the values making up the chart are taken at every 5-minute interval. Similarly, a wide variety of use cases, ranging from IOT sensors to application performance monitoring, all generate time-series data.

---

[4]Cardinality is a measure of the number of elements in a dataset.

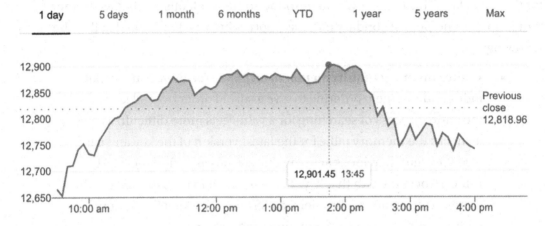

Figure 3-6. *NASDAQ over a 1-day period*

Time-series data is not just a collection of random samples in chronological order; rather, it is that data which gains significance when a time dimension is added to it. Time-series data usually exists at high levels of granularity such as milliseconds and microseconds, and the rate of change of the measured dimension is of interest to operations teams and application owners. It is used for both historical and real-time analysis, forecasting based on behavioral patterns, and detecting any anomalous spikes exhibited by the system. Two important characteristics of time-series data are

- **Immutability:** As time-series data always comes in order, each data point is recorded as a new entry and therefore is appended to the existing set of data. Once recorded, a data point usually never changes, and therefore time-series data is also called immutable data. Immutable time-series data is added sequentially as more time-series data gets generated. In contrast, a relational database is mutable, where database rows are frequently updated in response to the transactions.

- **Measured value:** The measured value of time-series data can be int64, float64, Boolean, or string and is not necessarily restricted to numerical data.

TSDB

Time-series data needs a purpose-built database which is designed to handle the ever-increasing massive amounts of timestamped metrics and events data. Most modern monitoring tools store monitoring data in a TSDB which is optimized to store timestamped data. Metrics and events that are timestamped can be easily stored, analyzed, and aggregated over time in this database, whether it be server metrics, network flow data, sensor data, application performance monitoring data, clickstream data, events, or just about any kind of data having a time index. Once the data is stored in the TSDB it is easy to measure its rate of change.

Key properties of a TSDB are

- **High write throughput:** In a monitoring system, data is collected very frequently and then written to a database. The data is written more often than it is read from, with typically 90%-95% being write operations. Therefore, the back-end database should be able to support a very high number of write operations. TSDBs are designed for high concurrent writes and provide a very high write throughput.

- **Data summarization:** In a monitoring system, there are requests made for summarized data over a particular time range which can range from a few days to a few months. This is done to establish patterns and identify failures which might have gone unnoticed in the past. The database query can actually involve an inordinate amount of time-series data and the database should be able to aggregate all this data without any noticeable latency. In the case of a TSDB, a user can write interactive queries on the data and get results instantaneously without having to wait for data processing and data summarization. This is very difficult to achieve optimally using relational databases.

- **Data rollup and aggregation:** In a monitoring system, generally high-precision data that is a few days old is kept as is, whereas data which has become older is aggregated with fewer samples from the data retained. This is termed as downsampling. The benefit of a TSDB is that it can do data aggregation and rollup on its own and no complex procedure is needed to be maintained by the database admins.

- **Data comparison:** In a TSDB, every new entry and every change are appended only and added as a new row to measure the change with respect to time. This is useful to calculate variance with previously observed values.

- **Massive storage:** Another design consideration for a TSDB is to store a massive amount of information, sometimes even ranging to petabytes (PB) and at the same time to be able to support high availability and a distributed architecture to be able to support multiple concurrent writes.

These are the some of the key design attributes of a TSDB. It can efficiently handle massive amounts of timestamped data while at the same time working on data management and summarization out of the box. By understanding the important characteristics of time-series data and the basic design principles behind a TSDB, we can clearly ascertain that NoSQL databases that use LSM-Tree–based storage engines have significant advantages over B-Tree–based relational database management systems.

LSM-Tree–based TSDBs, as we previously saw, are designed to optimize the writes, and in some cases their write performance reaches ten times higher when compared with B-Tree–based RDBMS. In contrast, their read performance is poor. LSM-Tree–based TSDBs are suited only for scenarios that are highly skewed towards writes rather than reads. Most of the well-known open source TSDBs use LSM-Tree–based storage engine; for instance, OpenTSDB uses HBase as the underlying storage engine, Prometheus relies on LSM-based LevelDB storage engine, and InfluxDB uses a Time Structured Merge (TSM) storage engine, which was developed on top of LSM. We will learn more about these storage engines when we discuss these specific open source tools in more detail in Part 2 of this book.

Time-Series Data Models

A time-series data model consists of the following:

- **Timestamp:** The time-indexed value for each data point measured.

- **Subject:** It refers to the component being measured; for example, in the case of CPU usage, the subject would be the host. A subject can further have multiple attributes and dimensions.

- **Measurement:** Measurement is the metric along with its value which we are trying to measure, which in the case of CPU can be CPU usage percentage or in the case of storage disk can be disk IOPS.

Modeling by Data Source

In this model, all metrics from a single data source at a given time are stored in the same row as fields. For example, in Figure 3-7, both CPU usage percentage and disk IOPS for host 1 are captured and entered as one single entry for the first timestamp at 14:00:00Z. This would help to write queries that join multiple fields under one single measurement.

Timestamp	Subject		Measurements	
timestamp	datacenter	hostname	cpu	disk iops
2020-08-26T 14:00:00Z	Datacenter 1	host 1	30	500
2020-08-26T 14:00:00Z	Datacenter 1	host 2	15	100
2020-08-26T 14:00:10Z	Datacenter 1	host 1	33	750
2020-08-26T 14:00:10Z	Datacenter 1	host 2	12	100
2020-08-26T 14:00:20Z	Datacenter 1	host 1	35	800
2020-08-26T 14:00:20Z	Datacenter 1	host 2	20	200
2020-08-26T 14:00:30Z	Datacenter 1	host 1	32	650
2020-08-26T 14:00:30Z	Datacenter 1	host 2	22	150

Figure 3-7. *Modeling by data source*

Modeling by Metrics

In the model shown in Figure 3-8, metrics drive the data point, as each row represents a certain metric and its measurement at a given time. For example, both CPU usage percentage and disk IOPS have a separate row entry for a given timestamp for host 1.

Metrics	Timestamp	Subject		Measurements
metric	timestamp	datacenter	hostname	metric value
cpu	2020-08-26T 14:00:00Z	Datacenter 1	host 1	30
cpu	2020-08-26T 14:00:00Z	Datacenter 1	host 2	15
cpu	2020-08-26T 14:00:10Z	Datacenter 1	host 1	33
cpu	2020-08-26T 14:00:10Z	Datacenter 1	host 2	12
cpu	2020-08-26T 14:00:20Z	Datacenter 1	host 1	35
cpu	2020-08-26T 14:00:20Z	Datacenter 1	host 2	20
cpu	2020-08-26T 14:00:30Z	Datacenter 1	host 1	32
cpu	2020-08-26T 14:00:30Z	Datacenter 1	host 2	22
disk iops	2020-08-26T 14:00:00Z	Datacenter 1	host 1	500
disk iops	2020-08-26T 14:00:00Z	Datacenter 1	host 2	100
disk iops	2020-08-26T 14:00:10Z	Datacenter 1	host 1	750
disk iops	2020-08-26T 14:00:10Z	Datacenter 1	host 2	100
disk iops	2020-08-26T 14:00:20Z	Datacenter 1	host 1	800
disk iops	2020-08-26T 14:00:20Z	Datacenter 1	host 2	200
disk iops	2020-08-26T 14:00:30Z	Datacenter 1	host 1	650
disk iops	2020-08-26T 14:00:30Z	Datacenter 1	host 2	150

Figure 3-8. *Modeling by metrics*

Data Analysis and Query Engine

Once the telemetry data has been collected and stored in the TSDB, the next step is to analyze the data. Common data analysis methods include filtering, aggregation, grouping, and downsampling. Data analysis is done through a query engine which can easily work on the stored data and provide the queried results. The query engines generally use queries that are modifications on top of SQL like query languages to query the data. In this section, we will look at the data analysis methods and also learn about the various mechanisms used to query telemetry data inside TSDBs.

Filter

Filtering is the most common process in which we run a query on the complete dataset and it returns only those datapoints that match the conditions set out in the query. In the case of time-series analysis, the filtering starts from a metric value and then refines it for time range or measurements as per the query. In the following example for the sample time-series data, we first select the datapoints from the table with the metric 'cpu' and then perform a more detailed query based on other conditions such as 'datacenter' or 'hostname.'

In order to explain the concept of filtering, we are using the sample data shown in Figure 3-9:

metric	timestamp	datacenter	hostname	metric value
cpu	2020-08-26T 14:00:00Z	Datacenter 1	host 1	30
cpu	2020-08-26T 14:00:00Z	Datacenter 1	host 2	15
cpu	2020-08-26T 14:00:10Z	Datacenter 1	host 1	33
cpu	2020-08-26T 14:00:10Z	Datacenter 1	host 2	12
cpu	2020-08-26T 14:00:20Z	Datacenter 1	host 1	35
cpu	2020-08-26T 14:00:20Z	Datacenter 1	host 2	20
cpu	2020-08-26T 14:00:30Z	Datacenter 1	host 1	32
cpu	2020-08-26T 14:00:30Z	Datacenter 1	host 2	22
disk iops	2020-08-26T 14:00:00Z	Datacenter 1	host 1	500
disk iops	2020-08-26T 14:00:00Z	Datacenter 1	host 2	100
disk iops	2020-08-26T 14:00:10Z	Datacenter 1	host 1	750
disk iops	2020-08-26T 14:00:10Z	Datacenter 1	host 2	100
disk iops	2020-08-26T 14:00:20Z	Datacenter 1	host 1	800
disk iops	2020-08-26T 14:00:20Z	Datacenter 1	host 2	200
disk iops	2020-08-26T 14:00:30Z	Datacenter 1	host 1	650
disk iops	2020-08-26T 14:00:30Z	Datacenter 1	host 2	150

Figure 3-9. *Original sample data*

The query selects cpu from table where datacenter= 'Datacenter 1' and hostname= 'host 1'; when run on the preceding table, this will provide the table shown in Figure 3-10:

metric	timestamp	datacenter	hostname	metric value
cpu	2020-08-26T 14:00:00Z	Datacenter 1	host 1	30
cpu	2020-08-26T 14:00:10Z	Datacenter 1	host 1	33
cpu	2020-08-26T 14:00:20Z	Datacenter 1	host 1	35
cpu	2020-08-26T 14:00:30Z	Datacenter 1	host 1	32

Figure 3-10. *Filtered data*

The resulting table is filtered on the basis of datacenter and hostname to return results which satisfy the queried values equal to 'Datacenter 1' and 'host 1.' This is a simple example to show the mechanism of filtering telemetry data from a given dataset.

Aggregation

Time-series data has high cardinality as data points are collected and stored at time intervals as small as every minute or every few seconds. Sometimes the rate of change of this high-precision data is minimal over a particular time range, and therefore what we need is some aggregation involving the basic statistical functions such as SUM, AVG, Max, and TopN. For example, when analyzing the server traffic, we would be more interested in knowing the peak traffic, the average traffic, and the sum total over a time range.

Before we apply aggregation, let's first look again at the original data with which we are working here in Figure 3-11:

metric	timestamp	datacenter	hostname	metric value
cpu	2020-08-26T 14:00:00Z	Datacenter 1	host 1	30
cpu	2020-08-26T 14:00:00Z	Datacenter 1	host 2	16
cpu	2020-08-26T 14:00:10Z	Datacenter 1	host 1	33
cpu	2020-08-26T 14:00:10Z	Datacenter 1	host 2	13
cpu	2020-08-26T 14:00:20Z	Datacenter 1	host 1	36
cpu	2020-08-26T 14:00:20Z	Datacenter 1	host 2	20
cpu	2020-08-26T 14:00:30Z	Datacenter 1	host 1	32
cpu	2020-08-26T 14:00:30Z	Datacenter 1	host 2	22
disk iops	2020-08-26T 14:00:00Z	Datacenter 1	host 1	500
disk iops	2020-08-26T 14:00:00Z	Datacenter 1	host 2	100
disk iops	2020-08-26T 14:00:10Z	Datacenter 1	host 1	750
disk iops	2020-08-26T 14:00:10Z	Datacenter 1	host 2	100
disk iops	2020-08-26T 14:00:20Z	Datacenter 1	host 1	800
disk iops	2020-08-26T 14:00:20Z	Datacenter 1	host 2	200
disk iops	2020-08-26T 14:00:30Z	Datacenter 1	host 1	650
disk iops	2020-08-26T 14:00:30Z	Datacenter 1	host 2	150

Figure 3-11. *Original sample data*

The query select avg(cpu) from table group by 'datacenter' will return the result shown in Figure 3-12:

metric	timestamp	datacenter	metric value
cpu	2020-08-26T 14:00:00Z	Datacenter 1	23
cpu	2020-08-26T 14:00:10Z	Datacenter 1	23
cpu	2020-08-26T 14:00:20Z	Datacenter 1	28
cpu	2020-08-26T 14:00:30Z	Datacenter 1	27

Figure 3-12. *Aggregated data*

The results of the query in the column 'metric value' are simple averages of the cpu usage percentage value of host 1 and host 2. This is useful when you have several hosts in a cluster and looking at individual host cpu utilization percentages wouldn't be meaningful. This resulting table is better to understand that the average cpu utilization is around 25 for the entire datacenter considering all the hosts.

Grouping

Grouping is shown in the example in Figure 3-12, where high-precision time-series data is aggregated and grouped into low-precision results through real-time computation. Depending on the query, the underlying database, the time range, and the granularity, the process of computation can be very slow at times. Some TSDBs optimize this process by preaggregation of the data to generate faster results. This will avoid detailed computation during query processing.

Downsampling

Downsampling is the process of converting high-resolution time-series data into low-resolution time-series data. This process is also called as rollup. To understand this, think of raw data being collected every second but after a few days, per-second data may not be so relevant. Therefore, we can try to rollup this per-second data to per-minute data, thus saving on storage costs.

This might appear to be similar to grouping but, it isn't. In grouping, we group data from different dimensions without changing the time dimension. For example, if we look at the preceding grouping table, we have grouped data from host 1 and host 2 into a single data point for Datacenter 1; however, the timestamps are not modified. So, if the data was at an interval of 10 seconds, the resulting data from the process of grouping is also at an interval of 10 seconds, but the dimension becomes higher.

However, downsampling is to aggregate data of the same dimension at different time intervals, thereby making the time granularity of the converted data coarser, while retaining the dimensions. Let's look at an example to understand this concept better.

The example in Figure 3-13 is a simple example of downsampling, which downsamples 10-second resolution data to 30-second resolution data by calculating the statistical average. The original data consists of host 1 cpu utilization values at every 10-second interval.

metric	timestamp	datacenter	hostname	metric value
cpu	2020-08-26T 14:00:00Z	Datacenter 1	host 1	30
cpu	2020-08-26T 14:00:10Z	Datacenter 1	host 1	36
cpu	2020-08-26T 14:00:20Z	Datacenter 1	host 1	21
cpu	2020-08-26T 14:00:30Z	Datacenter 1	host 1	31
cpu	2020-08-26T 14:00:40Z	Datacenter 1	host 1	22
cpu	2020-08-26T 14:00:50Z	Datacenter 1	host 1	40

Figure 3-13. *Aggregated data*

In Figure 3-14, the preceding data when downsampled to a 30-second time interval is shown.

metric	timestamp	datacenter	hostname	metric value (avg)
cpu	2020-08-26T 14:00:00Z	Datacenter 1	host 1	29
cpu	2020-08-26T 14:00:30Z	Datacenter 1	host 1	31

Figure 3-14. *Downsampling from interval (10 seconds) to interval (30 seconds)*

Auto-rollup

Auto-rollup is the automatic process of downsampling without the need to run an explicit query. Some popular open source databases include a feature for auto-rollup of data like InfluxDB, KairosDB, and so forth.

Data Visualization

Data visualization is the graphical representation of metric, event, and log data collected from various systems. With data pouring in from multiple disparate systems, data visualization helps us to analyze all this information and interpret it in a way which can then be used to make critical decisions. Using visual elements like graphs and charts, we can easily understand hidden patterns, unusual trends, and outliers in the data. Once identified, it becomes easier to rectify the particular problem or set an alert to capture potential issues for future.

Graphs and charts are commonly used as visualization styles; however, these are not the only options available and, in a few cases, may not be even suited for some datasets. There are visualization methods which might be more suited to a certain dataset and immensely more helpful to articulate the desired information. Some of the common types of data visualization are listed here:

- Graphs

- Maps

- Charts

- Tables

- Infographics

- Dashboards

Observability, as the name suggests, is about observing the trends and patterns in the enormous amount of data generated, to ascertain the health and performance of your systems. In order to make this possible, data has to be easily interpretable, which can only happen with the right set of visualization tools that can provide meaningful human-readable insights. The data can be interpreted in many ways as well, which ultimately depends on the query being executed and the type of visualization it serves.

In this section, we will go into detail to understand the various types of time-series visualizations, what they can help us infer, which scenarios are best suited for which visualization types, and how to look at data being aggregated over space and time.

Line Graphs

Line graphs are the most common and often the default option for converting a metric into a graph. A line graph represents a trendline by joining the various data points collected across different time intervals over a selected time range. For example, if the metrics are collected every 10 seconds for server requests reaching four different web servers, the trendline for each of them would join the data points received at a regular interval of 10 seconds over a 1-hour time range, would look similar to the line graph shown in Figure 3-15:

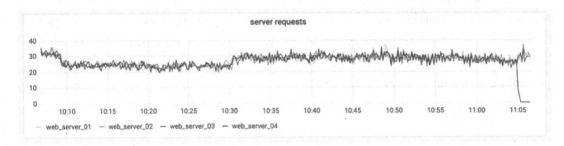

Figure 3-15. *Line graph of server requests to four web servers*

On close inspection, we can see that the line graph for one of the web servers, web_server_04, has dropped significantly at 11:05, which might mean that it was down at the time and was unable to serve requests. Since it is difficult to clearly see what is going on if the number of hosts is higher, we can isolate only the one web server we are interested in, in this case, web_server_04. The line graph for web_server_04 would look like the graph shown in Figure 3-16:

Figure 3-16. *Line graph of server requests to web_server_04*

The most common reason for using line graphs is to spot outliers quickly. In the preceding example, we can clearly see that the average server requests for web_server_04 is clearly an outlier at 11:05, as it dropped drastically from the average number of requests, which was hovering close to 30.

Figure 3-17. *Average server requests across all four web servers*

Another common usage is to aggregate the metrics received from all four web servers and see the line graph of the average server requests for all web servers combined. As shown in Figure 3-17, for the most part of the 1-hour time range under consideration, the server requests were averaging less than 30; however, there was some fluctuation around 11:50 which continued till 12:00 when the server requests increased to 40. This fluctuation can mean a spike in demand for the 10 minutes under consideration where the server requests were significantly higher than the average number of requests.

Stacked Graphs

Line graphs can be represented in another way by stacking them with each other to represent the sum and overall contribution of each part in a stacked graph. In Figure 3-18, the same metrics of server requests to four different web servers are stacked with each other.

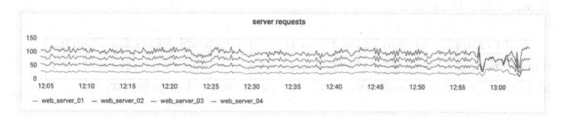

Figure 3-18. *Stacked graphs*

Stacked area graphs are similar to stacked graphs, where the graphs are represented by two-dimensional bands and not just lines. These are shown in Figure 3-19:

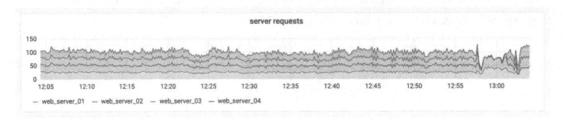

Figure 3-19. *Stacked area graphs*

Bar Graphs

When you present a metric rolled up over time as a bar, then this type of data visualization is called a bar graph, where each bar represents one or more metrics, which makes it suited for representing counts. Since a bar graph needs no interpolation from one data point to another, it is useful for representing sparse metrics or events that do not occur very frequently.

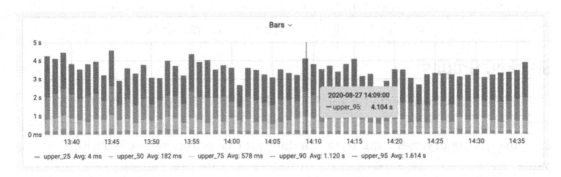

Figure 3-20. *Bar graph*

In the example shown in Figure 3-20, the stacked bar graph shows that 5% of the requests took an average of 1.614 s to get completed. The specific data point which is highlighted by the tool tip shows a particular request taking 4.104 s to complete.

Heatmaps

Heatmaps show the distribution of a single metric value, when collected from multiple sources, across different groups called buckets. The shading of each cell represents that for a given metric, and various different sources are reporting a particular value which corresponds to a defined bucket. The main use case for heatmaps is to convey general trends at a glance when a single metric is reported by multiple sources. This also represents any variations that don't correspond to what other group members might be reporting. An example of a heatmap is shown in Figure 3-21:

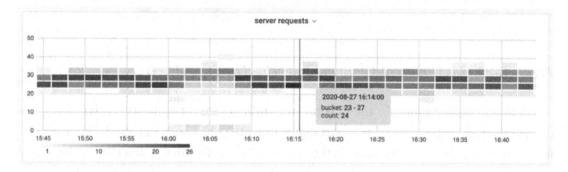

Figure 3-21. *Heatmap*

This heatmap represents the server requests received by the four web servers over a 1-hour time range. It shows that majority of the data points are in the range of 20-30, which means that there are about 20-30 server requests received by each web server every second on an average. If we focus on the highlighted cell, we can see that around 16:15 almost 24 data points were received by the webservers. We can also see some outliers around 16:05, which can be further investigated.

Summary Graphs

Summary graphs are visualizations that provide a summarized view rather than an elaborate time-series–based point-by-point analysis of all the data points. Summary graphs are useful in operation control centers, where information has to be displayed on monitors and elaborate graphs are not suitable for big-screen presentation. Aggregation is a good example of a summary graph.

Aggregation

When the data values are aggregated across time ranges by simply displaying only a single data point which can be a result of either a direct metric or a complex computation over that metric, that data visualization is said to be aggregated over time.

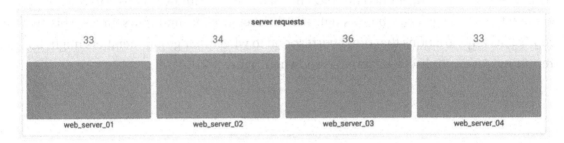

Figure 3-22. *Maximum server requests received by the web servers*

In the preceding example, the maximum number of server requests received by each of the four web servers over a particular time range has been depicted. While all four web servers received requests in the range of 30-35, we can see that the maximum requests came to web_server_03. In Figure 3-23, we are looking at the status codes generated due to the server requests received by a single server. We can see that there were 212 code_200 generated whereas there was only a single code_500 generated out of the total server requests over a 1-hour time period.

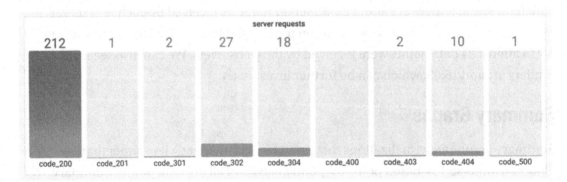

Figure 3-23. *Request status codes received by a single web server*

Alerting Engine

Alerting is the critical component of a monitoring system used to notify SREs about a drastic change in the state of a system. This notification is often sent to the operator through an integrated communication mechanism like SMS, email, call, or page, or as a ticket in the ticketing system. An alerting system, when successfully implemented, becomes an important part of an effective monitoring system. Let's first look at some of the basic concepts in alerting:

> **Alarm**: It describes any prominent change in a system's state, sometimes undesirable, by examining the fluctuations in data points received from the system.

> **Monitor**: Monitor is a threshold limit set for an alarm. A monitor evaluates a time series against the set threshold which consists of limits (upper or lower data points) for a specific duration. When the data points exceed the threshold or fall below the threshold for long enough, the threshold is said to be breached and the monitor triggers an alarm.

> **Alert**: An alert is a notification for an alarm, when a system transitions through a fluctuating state, breaching a threshold for a specific duration, and is detected by the configured monitor.

For example, an SRE may configure an alarm to alert himself when the system exceeds a monitor of 80% CPU utilization continuously for a period of 10 minutes. Before one can effectively start creating alerts, it is important to gather the information around system performance in normal conditions. This will then become the system's baseline performance for the creation of an initial alert configuration. Keeping the baseline in mind, you can then set a monitor for exceptional values that should actually correspond to an abnormal condition during its run in production. In hindsight, this monitor can then be scaled up or down to catch conditions not effectively tracked up till now. If this is not done, actual problems might go undetected and there might be a significant risk of complete shutdown. If a problem does get detected, as part of incident resolution, it is imperative to tweak the systems in order to avoid a reoccurrence and costly downtimes.

In an ideal scenario, alerts would get triggered only in response to an actual problem; however, that is not usually what happens. Multiple considerations such as the ones explained in the following make alerting a challenging practice to execute effectively:

- **Too conservative:** Operation teams tend to be more conservative when they set up alerts. This results in a deluge of alerts, as they keep getting triggered, resulting in alert fatigue. Too many alerts can lead to complacency within an operations team about false positives and ignoring critical alerts. This can lead to missing real problems, which ultimately defeats the purpose of alerting.

- **Optimum alert threshold:** Systems that are too sensitive can create false positives, and those that aren't can create false negatives, resulting in missing actual issues. Setting an optimum alert threshold comes with experience of running these systems in production and requires tuning and refinement on an ongoing basis.

- **Coverage:** Distributed systems scale quickly, and most often they are not covered under the gambit of effective alerting practices. This can result in teams missing out on the coverage of newer systems. Outdated alerts, if not updated regularly, can creep up and be difficult to manage over time, resulting in alert sprawl just like outdated firewall rules.

Modern distributed systems are more demanding and present unique problems for alerting:

- **Short lifespan:** Tracking any resource can be difficult when it is ephemeral in nature and readily appears and disappears on demand. Container orchestration tools like Kubernetes can spin up resources automatically to cater to change in CPU load. Therefore, monitoring CPU utilization in a containerized environment is rather less important than monitoring CPU saturation pattern.

- **Auto-discovery:** In cloud native environments, systems scale up and down rapidly. To cater to an unusual demand, there might be a momentary scale-up of resources, which can initiate an alert. However, by the time an operator looks at the dashboard, the scenario could be completely different. It is extremely difficult to do fault-finding for a scenario which happened momentarily and automation subsequently restored the systems back to normal behavior. Static alert policies are useless in an environment under constant change; therefore, alerting mechanisms should dynamically adjust to the current environment.

- **Managed services:** Due to developers relying on more and more managed services available from cloud infrastructure providers, the common operations responsibilities of operations teams are increasingly getting abstracted. Operation teams now need alerting higher up the stack to monitor and alert on business KPI performance.

Most organizations tend to put alerts on a variety of parameters; however, most alerts do not warrant an immediate human intervention. For example, in case CPU utilization of a container pod increases drastically, you would not want to put an alert on that event, as Kubernetes will bring the utilization levels down by initiating autoscaling. It is therefore very important to identify where to put an alert and at what threshold. In a distributed system, setting up alerts on resources is not advisable as the resources will always be in a flux. You need a different strategy to win the battle of alerts. In the next section, we will take a look at an effective alerting strategy for modern workloads.

Alerting Strategy

An effective alerting strategy can bring significant benefits to an organization and help in running your operations efficiently. It is worthwhile to set up alerts on your systems and modify them as needed in order to effectively refine your alerting strategy. As a starting point, you can

- Identify a set of systems that are mission critical for the business

- Set up alerts on these systems and review them time to time for effectiveness

- Review your incident life-cycle process as part of any active incident retrospective

- Include alert reviews and tuning in an ongoing process for iteration and improvement

Some of the most important factors that should always be kept in mind while creating an effective alerting strategy are the following:

- **Put quality over quantity**: Successful SRE teams often have high-quality, more meaningful, but very few alert rules in place. Those teams that start with a "capture all" philosophy will accumulate low-quality, very frequent alerts that end up being noisy and less useful.

- **Set up actionable alerts**: Quality alert rules are actionable and generate alerts in situations that require active engagement and response; otherwise, they create needless alert fatigue. Meaningless alerting rules can function as a constant stream of nonactionable notifications that can frustrate the operators, and they end up ignoring all alerts. If nothing is wrong, there shouldn't be any noise from alerts.

- **Incident correlation and AIOps**: AIOps can help reduce noise and resolve issues faster. AIOps can identify meaningful context and help prioritize incidents that need the most attention. This works well when you ingest incident events from multiple sources, enrich incident data with meaningful context, and group to correlate related events. Based on the context and the related errors getting generated, AIOps can indicate who from the team of SREs should respond to that particular alert.

- **Dependency analysis:** It is important to determine if the dependencies are actionable or not in a failure scenario. If there is a failure in an upstream component resulting in downtime for your component, you might not be able to action the alert since you don't own the dependency and the upstream component. AIOps can help here by identifying the dependency of the component that failed and notifying the upstream owner of the failure of the particular component as well as the services to which it is related.

- **Alert automation:** To some alerts, you can associate an automated trigger to execute scripts that take care of the problem by itself rather than notifying an operator for manual intervention. You can automate your policies, notification channels, and incident tracking. The time you spend doing this upfront will save you time later during an actual outage.

- **Collaboration:** Collaboration is the cornerstone of an effective alerting strategy. If all team members understand the incident response policies and document troubleshooting steps, it can help prevent similar types of incidents from occurring in the future and resolve problems faster rather than reinventing the wheel. AIOps can help by learning from alert data and past experiences and automatically surfacing recommendations, the next time a similar event occurs.

Features of a Modern Alerting System

Cloud native containerized environments, where systems change constantly, need a different strategy for alert management. As more and more systems are added and these systems scale, alert management has to evolve beyond a set of naming conventions. It is important that these new systems are also included in the modified alerting strategy and all alerts are correctly applied across the right set of systems. Here are some methods for handling alerts in dynamic environments:

- **Label your systems:** When you label your applications and systems with a set of key/value pairs, you can automatically push alerts against these labels. When you add or change any alert policy, rather than individually applying it to all the components, all the components with a particular label can inherit the modified alert policy. When new systems or applications are added, they also acquire the same alert policy as intended for those with the same set of labels. For example, when you modify a policy under the "production" label, those changes are propagated across all apps with the same label, which is significantly more reliable than manually updating the policies for each app.

- **Use API for alerts:** APIs are an effective way to create, modify, and manage alerts. When you provision your systems using a configuration management tool like Chef, Puppet, or Ansible, you can integrate alerting endpoints to these systems to ensure that alert policies are programmatically created alongside the resources you provision with these tools. This will automate the process of creating and updating alerts and helps implement a consistent set of alert policies based on the workloads under consideration.

- **Alert as a Code:** Infrastructure as a Code (IaaC) has revolutionized the way DevOps teams provision, configure, and manage infrastructure systems. Extending the same principles to the field of alerts, you can automate your alerting system by defining your alerts in code. This is really advantageous, as now you can check your alerting rules into source control for versioning and backup; it now can serve as a documented reference and be standardized across systems. While it might require some prework to programmatically build out your alert policies, the gains from the improved automation are often well worth the time, especially for the most dynamic and complex systems.

Log Aggregation

Logging is another critical pillar of a modern monitoring system. Logs have been in use traditionally for a long time and are very useful in debugging problems and doing root cause analysis (RCA). Elaborate syslog implementations are regularly mounted in production to generate detailed logs for both infrastructure systems and applications. Application logs help us in understanding the intricacies of the way an application is performing, whereas infrastructure logs capture system-related information. As we saw earlier, the world of cloud native is completely different and therefore presents new challenges.

Challenges with logging:

- In a microservices application, there are many individual components and each component generates its own set of log data. With the increased set of components, the logs generated are also more than the usual amount. The challenge of scale is common in a logging environment.

- In a microservices application, multiple services are interdependent, and collecting the logs from a perspective of gaining understanding of the state of the service might not be enough. We would also need to look at the interaction logs in order to successfully trace the dependencies in between the services.

- The type of logs generated from each service may differ, which is yet another challenge, as the logging formats for each of the services may differ. This leads to inconsistency from the log management and indexing perspective.

- In a microservice application, one service might be running on a single on prem node, whereas other services might be running on cloud. This is advantageous for microservices and the business, but it makes operations and logging much more difficult, as a distributed application will generate logs in different places and the compilation of those logs can be a big challenge.

- Microservices are generally deployed on containers or serverless functions which lack in-built persistent storage capabilities. When a microservice is running in a containerized environment, the logs are also contained within, which means that when the container dies, the associated logs will also disappear unless periodically moved and stored separately.

For all the previously mentioned points, the approach taken for logging of microservices is in contrast with that of a monolith. In the next section, we will look at the architecture for log aggregation, which tries to solve the challenges mentioned earlier.

Log Aggregation Architecture

Most logging systems in the open source world have similar architecture. The components described might have different names in different tools, but the function is more or less similar to what we describe in Figure 3-24:

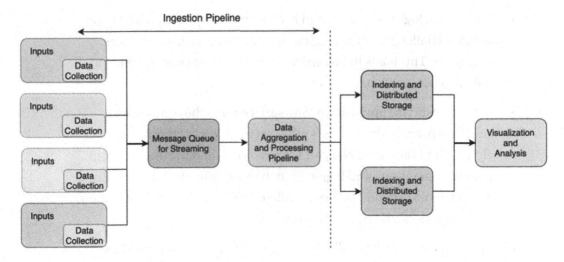

Figure 3-24. *Log aggregation architecture*

Ingestion Pipeline

An ingestion pipeline can be very basic or intricately complex, depending on the input sources and the log format they are generating. As we have seen previously in Chapter 2, log formats can be multiple, and this depends on the input sources which are generating that log.

The ingestion pipeline can have these components:

- **Data collection agent**: These are the agents which can be deployed on the nodes in your environment and work as log shippers for collecting logs or metrics. These are generally lightweight, with a small memory footprint and function with no dependencies.

- A popular open source log shipper is Beats from Elastic Stack, which is written in Go and collects different information as per the deployment. It can collect log files in the case of Filebeat, network data in the case of Packetbeat, system and service metrics in the case of Metricbeat, and so on.

- **Message queue:** Message queues buffer logs before they are indexed. They are placed in front of the critical data processing and indexing component in order to sustain the unexpected surge of logs in case of any event. The most commonly used message busses for this purpose are Kafka and Rabbit MQ.

- **Data aggregation and processing:** Efficient log processing is based
  on the structure of the logs. A well-defined structure makes it easier
  to search and analyze the log data. A well-defined log format will
  include application-level context and other details in order to make
  log data richer and more informative.

Logging in a Kubernetes Environment

Modern applications and container engines both support some kind of logging
mechanism. The standard method for containerized applications is to write logs to the
standard output (stdout) and standard error (stderr) streams. This, however, is a very
basic logging mechanism and will not suffice in case the container crashes or the node
dies; in such a case, the application logs will still be needed. It is suggested to have a
separate storage for logs that should be unrelated to the life cycle of nodes, pods, or
containers.

In the example shown in Figure 3-25, we will look at the basic logging functionality
available in Kubernetes that outputs data to the standard output stream. In the pod
specification file, **counter-pod.yaml**, we will create a pod named counter that writes
some text (date in this case) to standard output once per second.

```
1    apiVersion: v1
2    kind: Pod
3    metadata:
4      name: counter
5    spec:
6      containers:
7      - name: count
8        image: busybox
9        args: [/bin/sh, -c,
10              'i=0; while true; do echo "$i: $(date)"; i=$((i+1)); sleep 1; done']
```

Figure 3-25. *Pod specification for counter*

To run this pod, use the kubectl apply command:

```
$ kubectl apply -f counter-pod.yaml
```

The output of the command would be

```
pod/counter created
```

To fetch the logs, use the kubectl logs command:

```
$ kubectl logs counter
```

The output of this command is shown in Figure 3-26:

```
0:  Fri Aug 28 05:45:32 UTC 2020
1:  Fri Aug 28 05:45:33 UTC 2020
2:  Fri Aug 28 05:45:34 UTC 2020
3:  Fri Aug 28 05:45:35 UTC 2020
4:  Fri Aug 28 05:45:36 UTC 2020
5:  Fri Aug 28 05:45:37 UTC 2020
6:  Fri Aug 28 05:45:38 UTC 2020
7:  Fri Aug 28 05:45:39 UTC 2020
8:  Fri Aug 28 05:45:40 UTC 2020
9:  Fri Aug 28 05:45:41 UTC 2020
10: Fri Aug 28 05:45:42 UTC 2020
11: Fri Aug 28 05:45:43 UTC 2020
12: Fri Aug 28 05:45:44 UTC 2020
13: Fri Aug 28 05:45:45 UTC 2020
14: Fri Aug 28 05:45:46 UTC 2020
15: Fri Aug 28 05:45:47 UTC 2020
16: Fri Aug 28 05:45:48 UTC 2020
17: Fri Aug 28 05:45:49 UTC 2020
18: Fri Aug 28 05:45:50 UTC 2020
19: Fri Aug 28 05:45:51 UTC 2020
20: Fri Aug 28 05:45:52 UTC 2020
```

Figure 3-26. *Log data from counter*

Best Practices for Logging

We have seen the challenges with microservices-based logging and we have also looked at the modern log management solutions. Now let's learn a few best practices when it comes to logging cloud native applications in order to ensure that we can get complete visibility into those applications.

- **Centralized log aggregation**: In a microservices application, there are different places where the services are running and often generate various kinds of log data. It might seem easier to just run a distributed logging system which can collect logs locally instead of sending logs from multiple places into a single location. However, it is not feasible to manage and analyze logs which are spread out in terms of location and formats. Instead, it is advisable to deploy a centralized log aggregation system being fed by disparate input sources, so that we can correlate log data better.

- **Analyze all log data**: When you aggregate all log data at one place, you can run analysis on top of it and gain holistic visibility of the inner mechanisms of the system. Analyzing one service for its start time or the number of requests served is not very useful; rather, the correlation of this service with other services is what is meaningful to understand the application performance and availability.

- **Custom identifiers**: The log data generated by any application should include unique identifiers which can provide more information about the microservice that is generating the log. This information is very valuable as it can help contextualize the relevance of the log data as well as identify the interactions between multiple services. We would have to instrument the source code in order to include the custom identifiers in the log data. The second way is to offload this capability to agents which can also attach identifiers, such as tags, to log data without having to modify any code.

- **Custom parsing**: Log data generated by microservices can have different structures, and searching through it using generic regexes is ineffective. It is advisable to write custom parsing rules that can help identify the trends within log data even if their structures vary. With the use of custom log parsing, we can work with log data in any format without missing important insights.

- **Persist logs in external storage**: An effective best practice with respect to logging is to ensure that log data is written and stored in a place where it can be persisted and remains available even if the container shuts down. In order to do so, we can configure our container to send out logs to a common external storage either by modifying the source code or by running a logging agent.

Summary

Thankfully, there are several open source software tools which can help us navigate through this data and make sense of it. However, the challenge lies in selecting which one best suits your environment. In Part 2 of this book, we are going to take a deep dive into some of the most prominent open source monitoring solutions available and identify the problems they are trying to solve. We will also try to understand the difference in how they operate and why some of them might be suited to solve one particular problem and others might be well suited to solve another. In any case, organizations can build an effective monitoring strategy by combining several solutions together and correlating the information through a visualization platform. We will also look at a particular visualization platform in detail in Part 2 of this book.

PART II

Open Source Monitoring Tools

In Part 1 of this book, we discussed modern monitoring systems, their components, and their design. In Part 2, we will look at some of the popular monitoring tools which can help you achieve the observability goals we set out earlier. In the first three chapters, we have regularly mentioned tools like Prometheus, Grafana, ELK Stack, and so forth to explain certain concepts but haven't discussed them at length. In this part, we will explore these tools in detail. We start by installing them on a Kubernetes cluster first and then we use them to analyze the behavior of the cluster components themselves and the workloads that they are running.

In the next chapter, we look at Prometheus in detail to figure out if it can fulfill the criteria listed for modern monitoring systems in Chapter 3. We will learn about the use cases Prometheus is suited for and also the ones it is not suited for.

CHAPTER 4

Prometheus

Prometheus was first developed at SoundCloud in 2012. It was inspired by Google's approach to monitoring dynamic environments using Borgmon and was co-created by ex-Google SREs Matt Proud and Julius Volz, then working at SoundCloud. In 2016 it became the second project to graduate from CNCF after Kubernetes.

Before the genesis of Prometheus, SoundCloud was already running containers and was using an in-house Heroku-style cluster scheduler called Bazooka. They were using their old monitoring tools such as Nagios, StatsD, and Graphite to monitor this environment but were facing serious challenges. Nagios was used for fault detection and alerting but it lacked metrics history. It could only show how many times a check had failed. StatsD and Graphite do collect metric history but in the case of StatsD, if you wanted to collect any metrics from a process then you needed to send UDP packets from that process to StatsD. This meant that user traffic and monitoring traffic would go together, thus impacting each other. UDP packets don't come with guaranteed delivery; therefore, StatsD would easily miss out on reporting some data points as it would be unaware of missing UDP packets sporadically. Dimensionality was another area of concern as both StatsD and Graphite had a flat data model wherein there is a single metric name with dot-separated components. The query language of Graphite was not well suited to working with this data model and also run alerting on top of it. So, it was really difficult to find out, for example, if there was a latency spike, whether there were multiple instances involved, and specifically which ones were responsible for it.

Faced with these challenges and based on their experience at Google, the founders created Prometheus from the ground up, which was more suited for dynamic environments. Their approach was to collect all the metrics from a target system over HTTP and place it into a time-series database, as it is easier to aggregate, drill down, or slice and dice time-series data. It resulted in a simple yet effective data model which when combined with a powerful query language, is able to inspect how the applications and underlying infrastructure was behaving. For ad hoc debugging, you can use the

© Mainak Chakraborty and Ajit Pratap Kundan 2021
M. Chakraborty and A. P. Kundan, *Monitoring Cloud-Native Applications*,
https://doi.org/10.1007/978-1-4842-6888-9_4

default Prometheus UI, accessible over port 9090 on the Prometheus server, to try out the Prometheus query expressions. If you want to dashboard a certain expression, you can easily integrate with a visualization tool like Grafana, which can talk to Prometheus API and present you with nice dashboards. You can also use the same query language to formulate precise alerts on events which you need to be alerted about and then forward that alert to a specific notification system of your choice.

Prometheus is mostly written in Go with some components written in Java, Python, and Ruby, and it can be deployed as a single statically compiled binary with no other dependencies. It is licensed under the Apache 2.0 license. Prometheus was well received by the open source community, and an ecosystem of other tools has grown around it to support use cases which are currently not supported by Prometheus. Some of these tools, such as Cortex from WeaveWorks and Thanos, are currently sandbox projects within CNCF.

Installation

There are two choices to run Prometheus: one option is to run Prometheus on a separate dedicated node alongside the Kubernetes cluster, and the second option is to run it in the same node in which your other pods are running. These two deployment options are shown in Figure 4-1:

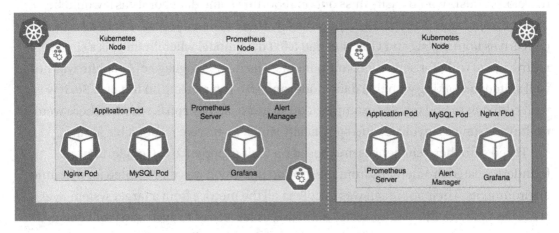

Figure 4-1. *Different deployment options for Prometheus*

There are pros and cons with both options. In the first option of stand-alone deployment, you have to take care of the networking between the nodes and configure Prometheus to collect the metrics from the other nodes that are present. This can be done by configuring a container networking platform like Flannel or Calico. In the second option of combined deployment, if you need to upgrade your pods, you also need to ensure that associated history is maintained and backed up, so that Prometheus doesn't lose the historical data during a rolling upgrade. Therefore, it is easier to run it alongside your workloads rather than as a separate setup if there are no other constraints. For the purposes of this book, we will follow the second option.

The installation steps mentioned in the following assumes that a Kubernetes cluster has already been set up. Readers are advised to use Minikube or Kind to setup a Kubernetes cluster by following instructions available at https://kubernetes.io/docs/tasks/tools/.

Once Minikube is installed, start the Kubernetes cluster (as shown in Figure 4-2) using the following command:

```
$ minikube start
```

```
mainakc ~ %minikube start
    minikube v1.12.3 on Darwin 10.15.7
    Using the docker driver based on existing profile
    minikube 1.16.0 is available! Download it: https://github.com/kubernetes/minikube/releases/tag/v1.16.0
    To disable this notice, run: 'minikube config set WantUpdateNotification false'

!   Requested memory allocation (1998MB) is less than the recommended minimum 2000MB. Kubernetes may crash unexpectedly.
!   Your system has 8192MB memory but Docker has only 2996MB. For a better performance increase to at least 3GB.

        Docker for Desktop  > Settings > Resources > Memory

    Starting control plane node minikube in cluster minikube
    Restarting existing docker container for "minikube" ...
    Preparing Kubernetes v1.18.3 on Docker 19.03.8 ...
    Verifying Kubernetes components...
    Enabled addons: dashboard, default-storageclass, storage-provisioner
    Done! kubectl is now configured to use "minikube"
```

Figure 4-2. Starting the single-node Kubernetes cluster

Once the Kubernetes cluster is up and running and kubectl has been installed successfully, the first thing to do is to list all the pods in the cluster (see Figure 4-3) using the following command:

```
$ kubectl get pods –all-namespaces
```

```
mainakc ~ %kubectl get pods --all-namespaces
NAMESPACE            NAME                                              READY   STATUS    RESTARTS   AGE
default              nginx-f89759699-5v46w                             1/1     Running   1          5d1h
kube-system          coredns-66bff467f8-n9jvm                          1/1     Running   1          5d3h
kube-system          etcd-minikube                                     1/1     Running   1          5d3h
kube-system          kube-apiserver-minikube                           1/1     Running   3          5d3h
kube-system          kube-controller-manager-minikube                  1/1     Running   5          5d3h
kube-system          kube-proxy-ghsd6                                  1/1     Running   1          5d3h
kube-system          kube-scheduler-minikube                           1/1     Running   2          5d3h
kube-system          storage-provisioner                               1/1     Running   5          5d3h
kubernetes-dashboard dashboard-metrics-scraper-dc6947fbf-g74dd         1/1     Running   1          5d3h
kubernetes-dashboard kubernetes-dashboard-6dbb54fd95-xcthl             1/1     Running   2          5d3h
```

Figure 4-3. *List of pods*

In Kubernetes, all the configurations are done using declarative constructs defined in a YAML (YAML Ain't Markup Language) file. For this installation also, we are going to use YAML files in order to explicitly define the configuration that we need, to run Prometheus on Kubernetes clusters. The first step is to create a separate namespace for our monitoring components. Namespaces are virtual clusters running on the same physical cluster that runs Kubernetes. This will ensure that we have our monitoring pods in a logically separate entity yet running on the same node as other workloads. You might notice in Figure 4-3 that there are already some namespaces defined—Kubernetes components are running in the 'kube-system' namespace and the nginx pod is running in a different namespace called 'default.'

We will create a new namespace called 'monitoring' using the YAML file, 'monitoring-namespace.yml.' This will create a separate namespace for monitoring, within which we will deploy all the components of our monitoring system. The YAML file is shown in Figure 4-4:

```
1 ---
2 apiVersion: v1
3 kind: Namespace
4 metadata:
5   name: monitoring
6
7 # create a new namespace called 'monitoring'
```

Figure 4-4. *monitoring-namespace.yml*

Open a text editor of your choice, paste the preceding configuration snippet into a file, and save it as 'monitoring-namespace.yml.' Then use the following command to create a new namespace (see Figure 4-5).

```
$ kubectl apply -f monitoring-namespace.yml
```

```
[mainakc ~/Book/Prometheus %kubectl apply -f monitoring-namespace.yml
namespace/monitoring created
```

Figure 4-5. *Creating a namespace*

Confirm that the list of namespaces (see Figure 4-6) includes the new monitoring namespace by using the following command:

```
$ kubectl get namespaces
```

```
[mainakc ~/Book/Prometheus %kubectl get namespaces
NAME                    STATUS    AGE
default                 Active    5d3h
kube-node-lease         Active    5d3h
kube-public             Active    5d3h
kube-system             Active    5d3h
kubernetes-dashboard    Active    5d3h
monitoring              Active    84s
```

Figure 4-6. *List of namespaces*

In the next step, we will create a ConfigMap which has the configuration data for running the Prometheus pods. It decouples the specific environmental configuration from the container images. Using the YAML file, prometheus-configmap.yaml shown in Figure 4-7, we will create a ConfigMap (see Figure 4-8) with name 'prometheus-config' in the namespace 'monitoring.' In the file, we are defining a scrape interval of 15 seconds and a job named 'Prometheus,' which will scrape the target (Prometheus itself) at port 9090 every 15 seconds to get metrics.

```
1 apiVersion: v1
2 kind: ConfigMap
3 metadata:
4    name: prometheus-config
5    namespace: monitoring
6 data:
7    prometheus.yml: |
8      global:
9        scrape_interval:        15s # Scrape every 15 seconds
10
11     # Scrape configuration - Scrape Prometheus itself
12
13     scrape_configs:
14
15       - job_name: 'prometheus'
16
17         static_configs:
18         - targets: ['localhost:9090']
```

Figure 4-7. *prometheus-configmap.yaml*

```
$ kubectl apply -f prometheus-configmap.yaml
```

```
[mainakc ~/Book/Prometheus %kubectl apply -f prometheus-configmap.yaml
configmap/prometheus-config_created
```

Figure 4-8. *Creating a ConfigMap*

In the next step, we are going to create a service account for Prometheus and bind it to a cluster role, which gives access to Prometheus to get all the metrics from resources (nodes, services, endpoints, pods) within the cluster and not just in the same 'monitoring' namespace. The YAML file to create these configurations is shown in Figure 4-9, and the execution for creating and binding is shown in Figure 4-10:

```
 1 ---
 2 apiVersion: rbac.authorization.k8s.io/v1beta1
 3 kind: ClusterRole
 4 metadata:
 5   name: prometheus
 6 rules:
 7 - apiGroups: [""]
 8   resources:
 9   - nodes
10   - nodes/proxy
11   - services
12   - endpoints
13   - pods
14   verbs: ["get", "list", "watch"]
15 - apiGroups:
16   - extensions
17   resources:
18   - ingresses
19   verbs: ["get", "list", "watch"]
20 - nonResourceURLs: ["/metrics"]
21   verbs: ["get"]
22 ---
23 apiVersion: v1
24 kind: ServiceAccount
25 metadata:
26   name: default
27   namespace: monitoring
28 ---
29 apiVersion: rbac.authorization.k8s.io/v1beta1
30 kind: ClusterRoleBinding
31 metadata:
32   name: prometheus
33 roleRef:
34   apiGroup: rbac.authorization.k8s.io
35   kind: ClusterRole
36   name: prometheus
37 subjects:
38 - kind: ServiceAccount
39   name: default
40   namespace: monitoring
```

Figure 4-9. *prometheus-roles.yml*

```
$ kubectl apply -f prometheus-roles.yml
```

```
mainakc ~/Book/Prometheus %kubectl apply -f prometheus-roles.yml
clusterrole.rbac.authorization.k8s.io/prometheus created
Warning: kubectl apply should be used on resource created by either kubectl create --save-config
or kubectl apply
serviceaccount/default configured
clusterrolebinding.rbac.authorization.k8s.io/prometheus created
```

Figure 4-10. *Creating a service account and bind with a cluster role*

Now we are ready to deploy Prometheus using the deployment YAML configuration mentioned in Figure 4-11. There are two specifications (spec) sections mentioned in the configuration. In the first specification, we will define the number of "replicas" to be created in a ReplicaSet, which in this case is set to 1. We also define the update "strategy" as type "RollingUpdate" and the "selector" to match the label - 'Prometheus' on the pods in order for ReplicaSet to know which pods to manage.

```
 1 ---
 2 apiVersion: apps/v1
 3 kind: Deployment
 4 metadata:
 5   name: prometheus
 6   namespace: monitoring
 7   labels:
 8     app: prometheus
 9 spec:
10   replicas: 1
11   strategy:
12     rollingUpdate:
13       maxSurge: 1
14       maxUnavailable: 1
15     type: RollingUpdate
16   selector:
17     matchLabels:
18       app: prometheus
19   template:
20     metadata:
21       labels:
22         app: prometheus
23       annotations:
24         prometheus.io/scrape: "true"
25         prometheus.io/port: "9090"
26     spec:
```

Figure 4-11. *prometheus-deployment.yaml*

```
27        containers:
28        - name: prometheus
29          image: quay.io/prometheus/prometheus:v2.0.0
30          imagePullPolicy: IfNotPresent
31          args:
32            - '--storage.tsdb.retention=6h'
33            - '--storage.tsdb.path=/prometheus'
34            - '--config.file=/etc/prometheus/prometheus.yml'
35          command:
36          - /bin/prometheus
37          ports:
38          - name: web
39            containerPort: 9090
40          volumeMounts:
41          - name: config-volume
42            mountPath: /etc/prometheus
43          - name: data
44            mountPath: /prometheus
45        restartPolicy: Always
46        securityContext: {}
47        terminationGracePeriodSeconds: 30
48        volumes:
49        - name: config-volume
50          configMap:
51            name: prometheus-config
52        - name: data
53          emptyDir: {}
```

Figure 4-11. *(continued)*

Lastly, we have the "template" section, which has the configuration of the pod defined. In the second spec section, we define the name of the pod, the image that will be deployed on the pod, and where to pull it from. Certain arguments like the location of the config file are also defined. The section on ports defines the container port 9090, which is open for web traffic. The volumeMounts section has two volumes specified: one for the Config and the other for data. Now let's deploy this YAML file using the following command (see Figure 4-12):

```
$ kubectl apply -f prometheus-deployment.yaml
```

```
[mainakc ~/Book/Prometheus %kubectl apply -f prometheus-deployment.yaml
deployment.apps/prometheus created
```

Figure 4-12. *Creating a deployment*

In order to verify what components have been created by the Prometheus deployment, we can use the following command (see Figure 4-13):

```
$ kubectl get all -namespace=monitoring
```

```
mainakc ~/Book/Prometheus %kubectl get all --namespace=monitoring
NAME                              READY    STATUS     RESTARTS    AGE
pod/prometheus-7f567bc485-4fjkr   1/1      Running    0           2m57s

NAME                           READY    UP-TO-DATE    AVAILABLE    AGE
deployment.apps/prometheus     1/1      1             1            2m57s

NAME                                      DESIRED   CURRENT   READY   AGE
replicaset.apps/prometheus-7f567bc485     1         1         1       2m57s
```

Figure 4-13. *List of resources in the monitoring namespace*

Since we don't have access to the resources that we created in the deployment, we will create a NodePort service that will provide us with the access to Prometheus. See Figure 4-14:

```
1 apiVersion: v1
 2 kind: Service
 3 metadata:
 4   name: prometheus
 5   namespace: monitoring
 6 spec:
 7   selector:
 8     app: prometheus
 9   type: NodePort
10   ports:
11   - name: prometheus
12     protocol: TCP
13     port: 9090
14     nodePort: 30900
```

Figure 4-14. *prometheus-nodeservice.yaml*

Let us deploy this file and create the NodePort service using the following command (see Figure 4-15):

```
$ kubectl apply -f prometheus-nodeservice.yaml
```

```
[mainakc ~/Book/Prometheus %kubectl apply -f prometheus-nodeservice.yaml
 service/prometheus created _
```

Figure 4-15. *Creating a Nodeservice*

NodePort exposes the service on each node's IP at a static port (NodePort) with default value, which is usually between 30000 and 32767. We can now look at Prometheus on port 30900 of the single node and use the following command to open Prometheus in a web browser.

```
$ minikube service –namespace=monitoring prometheus
```

The output of the command is shown in Figure 4-16:

```
mainakc ~/Book/Prometheus %minikube service --namespace=monitoring prometheus
|-------------|-------------|-------------------|----------------------------|
| NAMESPACE   |    NAME     |    TARGET PORT    |            URL             |
|-------------|-------------|-------------------|----------------------------|
| monitoring  | prometheus  | prometheus/9090   | http://172.17.0.2:30900    |
|-------------|-------------|-------------------|----------------------------|
🏃  Starting tunnel for service prometheus.
|-------------|-------------|-------------------|----------------------------|
| NAMESPACE   |    NAME     |    TARGET PORT    |            URL             |
|-------------|-------------|-------------------|----------------------------|
| monitoring  | prometheus  |                   | http://127.0.0.1:52677     |
|-------------|-------------|-------------------|----------------------------|
🎉  Opening service monitoring/prometheus in default browser...
❗  Because you are using a Docker driver on darwin, the terminal needs to be open to run it.
```

Figure 4-16. *Getting the URL to access Prometheus*

You should see this screen as the first screen after successful installation of Prometheus, as shown in Figure 4-17:

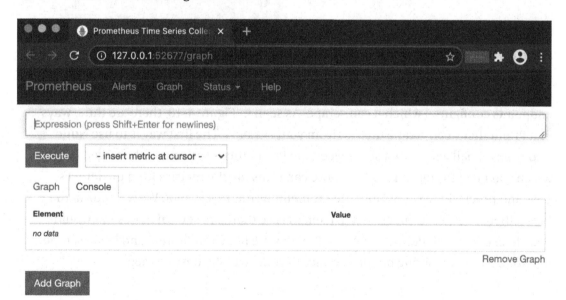

Figure 4-17. *Prometheus is now running*

This completes the section on Prometheus installation. Another easier way of installing Prometheus is by using Helm charts, which can simplify the process mentioned previously.

Architecture

We can break the components of Prometheus into four different categories: data collection, data storage, visualization, and alerting. This will make the entire architecture easy to understand and remember.

Data Collection

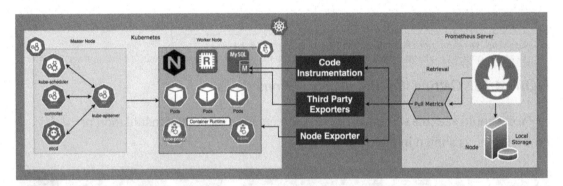

Figure 4-18. *Different methods of data collection using Prometheus*

Prometheus is essentially a pull-based system, which means that you need to have HTTP endpoints configured which it can scrape. As seen in Figure 4-18, there are three ways that Prometheus can scrape metrics from your systems. The first way is to use **Node Exporters**, small agents that sit between the Prometheus server and the target, from which you need to collect metrics. These can translate the metrics from the target's sysfs and procfs file systems[1] into the Prometheus metrics format. We will look at the Prometheus metrics format in detail later. In case there are several nodes, we would need to explicitly tell Prometheus which nodes are to be monitored, and it will scrape the Node Exporters sitting on those nodes to collect all the desired metrics.

---

[1] *procfs* or */proc* is a Linux filesystem that presents information about kernel processes. Newer Linux distributions use *sysfs* or */sys* to export information from the kernel.

The second way is to use third-party exporters, which can help in converting existing metrics from third-party systems to the Prometheus metrics format. These exporters are available for a wide variety of systems starting from databases, messaging systems, hardware, storages, and proxies and even other monitoring systems. Some of these exporters are created and supported officially and maintained in the Prometheus GitHub page, while others are created by third parties and maintained by them. For example, a MySQL exporter can use SQL queries to query a MySQL daemon, gather all the information, and then translate it to the Prometheus metrics format. There are several popular third-party software systems, such as Kubernetes, Linkerd, Docker daemon, and Telegraf, which expose metrics out of the box in the Prometheus format, and therefore no separate exporter is needed for these.

The third and the most important way is of instrumenting your code to send metrics to Prometheus is by using one of the client libraries. Officially supported client libraries include Go, Java, Python, and Ruby, and there are several unofficial third-party client libraries that you can choose from. Once you define the metrics you need, you can then expose these metrics over an HTTP endpoint. When Prometheus scrapes the instance on which the application is running, the client library sends the current state metrics on that HTTP endpoint.

There is a performance implication of instrumentation which can vary depending on the client library and the language used. Introducing a counter/gauge with a Java client can introduce a 12-17ns delay, depending on contention, which is negligible in most cases.

Exposition Format

The process of making metrics available to Prometheus is called exposition. Prometheus metrics exposed from any exporter or through code instrumentation can be found in the /metrics path in a text-based exposition format. Before v2.0, Prometheus supported another format based on protocol buffers (Protobuf) apart from the text-based format. Since v2.0, the Protobuf format is no longer supported. The advantages of a text-based format are that it is human-readable and easy to understand.

Prometheus metric types such as counter, gauge, histogram, summary, and untyped[2] can help you track the state of your environment. The text format is line oriented, wherein lines are separated by a line feed character (\n). The output generally includes a line that starts with a # as the first character, which is considered as a comment except

---

[2]Metric types were introduced in Chapter 2.

when the first character after # is either HELP or TYPE. HELP is a description of the metric and remains same irrespective of the TYPE of the metric. TYPE represents the type of the metric, which can be one of these: counter, gauge, histogram, summary, and untyped. Untyped is used when the metric type is unknown.

If the character after # is HELP, it is followed by the metric name. For a given metric, there can only be one line with HELP. If the character after # is TYPE, then it is succeeded by the metric name and the expected type of the metric. Similar to a HELP line, there can only be one TYPE line for a given metric. If in case there is no defined type of metric in a TYPE line, the TYPE is automatically set to untyped. The text format syntax is as follows:

```
metric_name [
  "{" label_name "=" `"` label_value `"` { "," label_name "=" `"`
  label_value `"` } [ "," ] "}"
] value [ timestamp ]
```

Metric name: This is the name of the metric, which is generally a description giving more information about the metric itself. Metric names are usually kept unique to avoid duplication among the libraries. It refers to a specific line of code in a particular file in a specific library from where the metric has to be collected.

Labels: More than one label can be included, separated by a comma; however it is important to have a consistent order from one scrape to another. For example:

```
# HELP counter_metric Just an example of counter
# TYPE counter_metric counter
counter_metric_total{foo="bar",baz="qux"} 2520
counter_metric_total{foo="bar",baz="qux"} 219
```

Timestamp: Timestamp is an integer value in milliseconds and is auto-applied by Prometheus after the value.

Figure 4-19 shows the HELP line, the TYPE line, and the counter metrics:

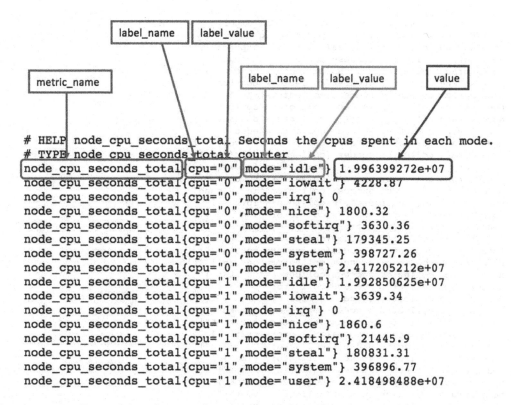

Figure 4-19. *Exposition format for a counter metric*

Figure 4-20 shows the HELP line, the TYPE line, and the gauge metrics:

```
# HELP node_scrape_collector_success node_exporter: Whether a collector succeeded.
# TYPE node_scrape_collector_success gauge
node_scrape_collector_success{collector="arp"} 1
node_scrape_collector_success{collector="bcache"} 1
node_scrape_collector_success{collector="bonding"} 1
node_scrape_collector_success{collector="conntrack"} 1
node_scrape_collector_success{collector="cpu"} 1
node_scrape_collector_success{collector="cpufreq"} 1
node_scrape_collector_success{collector="diskstats"} 1
node_scrape_collector_success{collector="edac"} 1
node_scrape_collector_success{collector="entropy"} 1
node_scrape_collector_success{collector="filefd"} 1
node_scrape_collector_success{collector="filesystem"} 1
node_scrape_collector_success{collector="hwmon"} 1
node_scrape_collector_success{collector="infiniband"} 1
node_scrape_collector_success{collector="ipvs"} 1
node_scrape_collector_success{collector="loadavg"} 1
node_scrape_collector_success{collector="mdadm"} 1
node_scrape_collector_success{collector="meminfo"} 1
node_scrape_collector_success{collector="netclass"} 1
node_scrape_collector_success{collector="netdev"} 1
node_scrape_collector_success{collector="netstat"} 1
node_scrape_collector_success{collector="nfs"} 1
node_scrape_collector_success{collector="nfsd"} 1
node_scrape_collector_success{collector="pressure"} 1
node_scrape_collector_success{collector="sockstat"} 1
node_scrape_collector_success{collector="stat"} 1
node_scrape_collector_success{collector="textfile"} 1
node_scrape_collector_success{collector="time"} 1
node_scrape_collector_success{collector="timex"} 1
node_scrape_collector_success{collector="uname"} 1
node_scrape_collector_success{collector="vmstat"} 1
node_scrape_collector_success{collector="xfs"} 1
node_scrape_collector_success{collector="zfs"} 1
```

Figure 4-20. *Exposition format for a gauge metric*

Figure 4-21 shows the HELP line, the TYPE line, and the summary metrics:

```
# HELP go_gc_duration_seconds A summary of the GC invocation durations.
# TYPE go_gc_duration_seconds summary
go_gc_duration_seconds{quantile="0"} 1.0783e-05
go_gc_duration_seconds{quantile="0.25"} 1.6019e-05
go_gc_duration_seconds{quantile="0.5"} 3.7685e-05
go_gc_duration_seconds{quantile="0.75"} 8.7524e-05
go_gc_duration_seconds{quantile="1"} 0.014988136
go_gc_duration_seconds_sum 1624.240639472
go_gc_duration_seconds_count 4.577738e+06
```

Figure 4-21. *Exposition format for a summary metric*

Figure 4-22 shows the HELP line, the TYPE line, and the untyped metrics:

```
# HELP node_vmstat_pgpgin /proc/vmstat information field pgpgin.
# TYPE node_vmstat_pgpgin untyped
node_vmstat_pgpgin 4.64097761e+08
# HELP node_vmstat_pgpgout /proc/vmstat information field pgpgout.
# TYPE node_vmstat_pgpgout untyped
node_vmstat_pgpgout 2.135340909e+09
```

Figure 4-22. *Exposition format for an untyped metric*

Service Discovery

Service discovery, as the name suggests, is concerned with the process of discovering the endpoints for scraping by Prometheus.

In order to scrape a target, you have to first configure the scrape_configs section in the prometheus.yml file with a defined job_name, the target host, and the port number. For example, Prometheus can scrape the Prometheus server essentially itself, just by adding the corresponding job_name in the scrape_configs section, as shown in Figure 4-23:

```
1  scrape_configs:
2   - job_name: prometheus
3     static_configs:
4      - targets:
5         - localhost:9090
```

Figure 4-23. *Static configuration*

For all the targets that you want to monitor, you can define the respective job name and then list them one by one in the YAML file. However, doing this manual addition in a dynamic environment where monitoring targets are ephemeral is not practical. To solve this particular challenge, Prometheus uses service discovery and supports discovering targets dynamically using any of the supported service discovery mechanisms such as Consul, DNS, Openstack, Kubernetes, EC2, Azure, and GCE. In case your preferred option is not supported, you can also use file-based service discovery.

Service discovery can be classified into two categories. One is where the instances register themselves with a service discovery mechanism such as Consul. This is called bottom-up service discovery. The second is when the service discovery tool finds out which instances there are, as in the case of EC2, which is termed top-down service discovery. The first method involves a reconciliation process to ensure that all the instances are registered, even if they shut down before they can be discovered. In the second method, since the service discovery tools know which instances are spawned, it can easily tell if the instance is down and unreachable.

Targets

For the first installation, you might be interested to see the targets Prometheus has been configured to collect the metrics from. To make things simple, it is preconfigured to collect metrics from the Prometheus server itself. You can navigate to Targets from the Status drop-down menu, as shown in Figure 4-24:

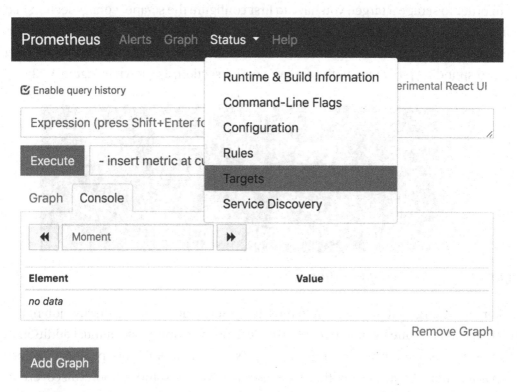

Figure 4-24. *Targets*

Once you are at the targets page, you can see that the screen shows the Prometheus server as a target and lets you know if it is up and running, which must be the case, since you are seeing the Prometheus UI. It also shows the labels associated with the server, in this case, Job and Instance. Apart from this information, you can also see when the last scrape happened and how much time it took to complete the scrape. All your targets will appear here, and you can check if they are sending metrics to the Prometheus server or not. See Figure 4-25.

Figure 4-25. *List of targets*

We have learned about service discovery in Section 2, and one can check for service discovery under the Status drop-down menu, as shown in Figures 4-26 and 4-27:

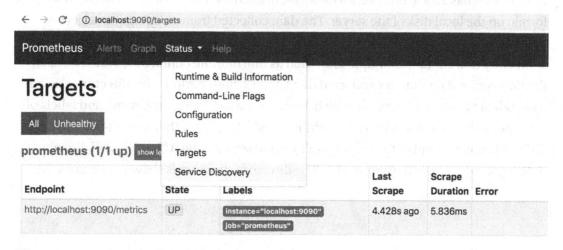

Figure 4-26. *Service discovery*

Figure 4-27. *Service discovery of target labels*

To understand this better, let's have a look at the prometheus.yml file. In the yaml file, we can define the target as localhost:9090. If there are more targets which need to be discovered, they can be added to the list in a similar way.

Data Storage

Prometheus has a local time-series database that stores time-series data in a custom format on the local disk of the server. The data collected from scraping the targets is first grouped into blocks of 2 hours each and stored in memory. Each block consists of a directory that contains multiple files, such as one or more chunk files, which have all the time-series data samples collected during the 2-hour period. This directory also has a metadata file and an index file, which includes the index of metric name and labels of the time-series samples stored in the chunk files. There is another file called tombstone file that keeps a record of the deletion of the time series using API, instead of directly deleting the data from the chunk files. The directory structure is shown in Figure 4-28:

Figure 4-28. *Data directory structure*

In Figure 4-28, you can clearly see the data directory structure with multiple folders of 2-hour blocks worth of data (see Figure 4-29). Since this data is not persisted yet, a log is maintained which can be replayed in case the Prometheus server fails and has to be restarted again. This log file is called the write ahead log (WAL) file and is stored in the wal directory in segments of 128MB.

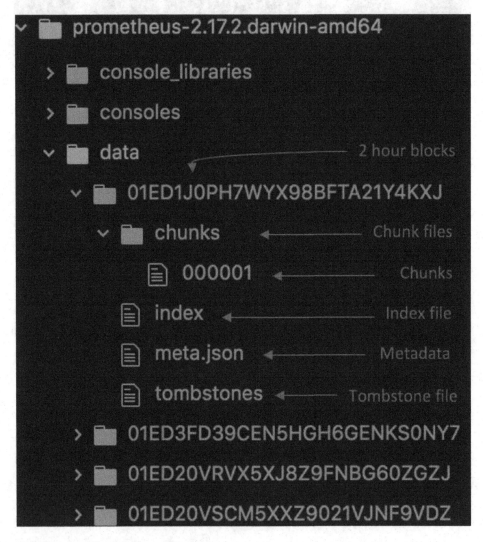

Figure 4-29. *Inside the data directory*

Capacity planning for the Prometheus server can easily be done by using the following formula:

Disk Space Needed = Ingested Samples/second*Bytes/Sample* Retention Time Period (in seconds)

Prometheus uses 1-2 bytes per sample, so in order to effectively control the disk space needed, you can adjust the ingestion rate by reducing the number of samples. This can be done either by reducing the number of targets that are to be scraped, or by collecting fewer samples from the target, or else by increasing the scrape interval. There are several ways to configure the local storage by using flags, as shown below:

Flag	Description	Default
`--storage.tsdb.path`	Path where to write database	data/
`--storage.tsdb.retention.time`	Time period for data retention	15d
`--storage.tsdb.retention.size`	Maximum bytes that storage blocks can use Ex- 512MB	0
`--storage.tsdb.wal-compression`	Enables compression on WAL size	-

Since the Prometheus time-series database is stored in the local disk and is not clustered or replicated, to avoid data loss in case of node failure, it is prudent to design for the durability of the local disk. This can be achieved by using redundant array of independent disks (RAID) for disk availability in case of disk failure or data backup and replication in case of node failure. If you need a solution for clustered long-term storage, it can be achieved by using the remote-read and remote-write feature of Prometheus, which allows sending and receiving data samples to remote storage.

Visualization

Prometheus comes in-built with a basic visualization tool called Expression Browser, which is accessible at `http://localhost:9090/graph`. Expression Browser (see Figure 4-30) allows you to enter any ad hoc query and see the result in a table or in the form of a graph. Prometheus also comes bundled with a few console templates that can be used to create different consoles which are then served directly from the file system of the Prometheus server. It allows you to render customized web pages and do source control with the dashboards. Console templates are a powerful feature and are therefore recommended only for solving advanced use cases.

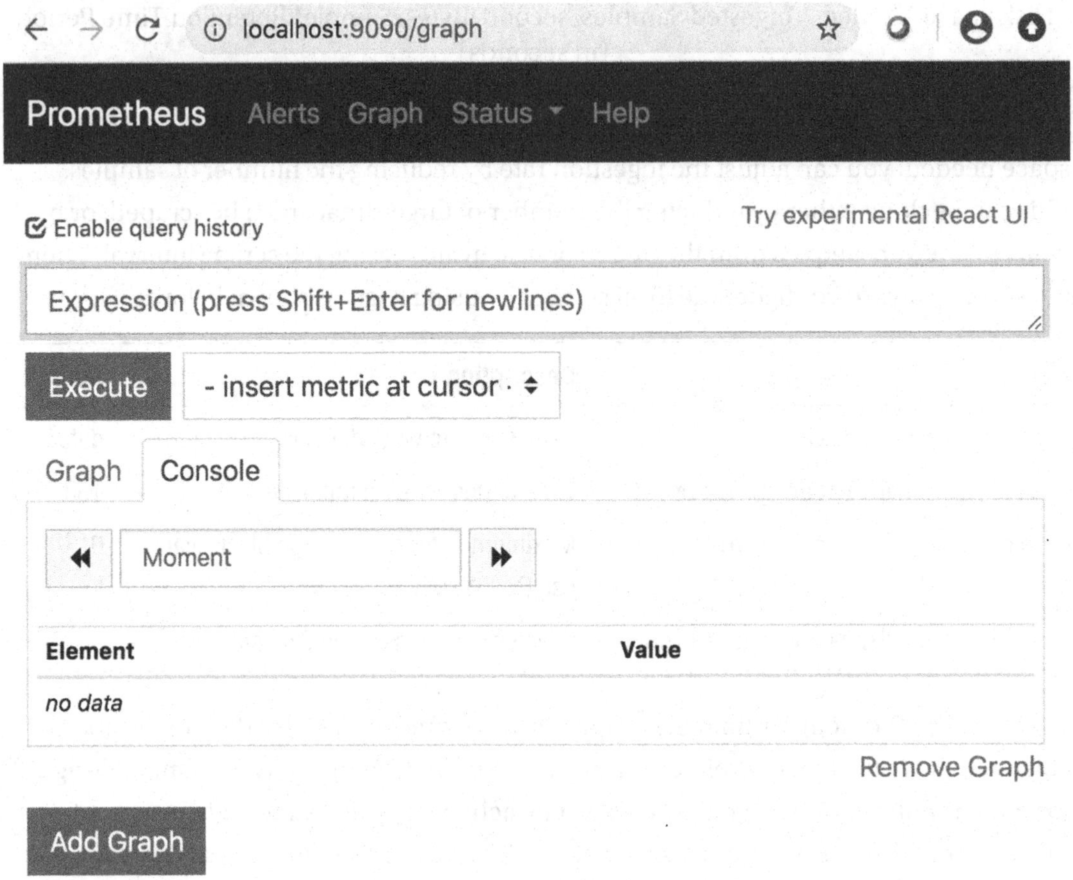

Figure 4-30.   *Expression Browser in the Classic UI*

Expression Browser has a central field where you can type any expression for quick debugging. You can also check a list of metrics that are discovered in the drop down menu: **Insert metric at cursor**, just next to the Execute button. At the bottom, there are two options to check the output of the expression which you executed previously. One option is the Console tab, which gives you the results, along with their labels of instance and jobs, and the corresponding value when the query was executed. The second option is the graph which charts out the variation of this value when reported over time.

It also lets you know three other relevant pieces of information:

1. Load Time

2. Resolution

3. Total Time Series

Let's try this with a query expression 'up'. Up is a metric which Prometheus adds by itself when it scrapes a target indicating whether Prometheus was able to successfully scrape the target or not. When we run this query in Expression Browser, we get two time-series data points, indicating that there are two targets which Prometheus has scraped and given us the results. If we refer to Figure 4-31, we can see that the two data points are coming from two different instances, which are localhost:9090 and localhost:9100. Instance here is a label which has been allocated to these targets, and there is another label called Job, which indicates the type of application the target is running. This configuration has to be done by a user in the prometheus.yml file in order to get this type of metadata in the results.

Since both the targets were successfully scraped, we can see a value of 1 assigned against these elements. If one of these were inaccessible and weren't reporting any metrics, this value would be 0. You can also check the three parameters of load time, resolution, and total time series mentioned for this query execution.

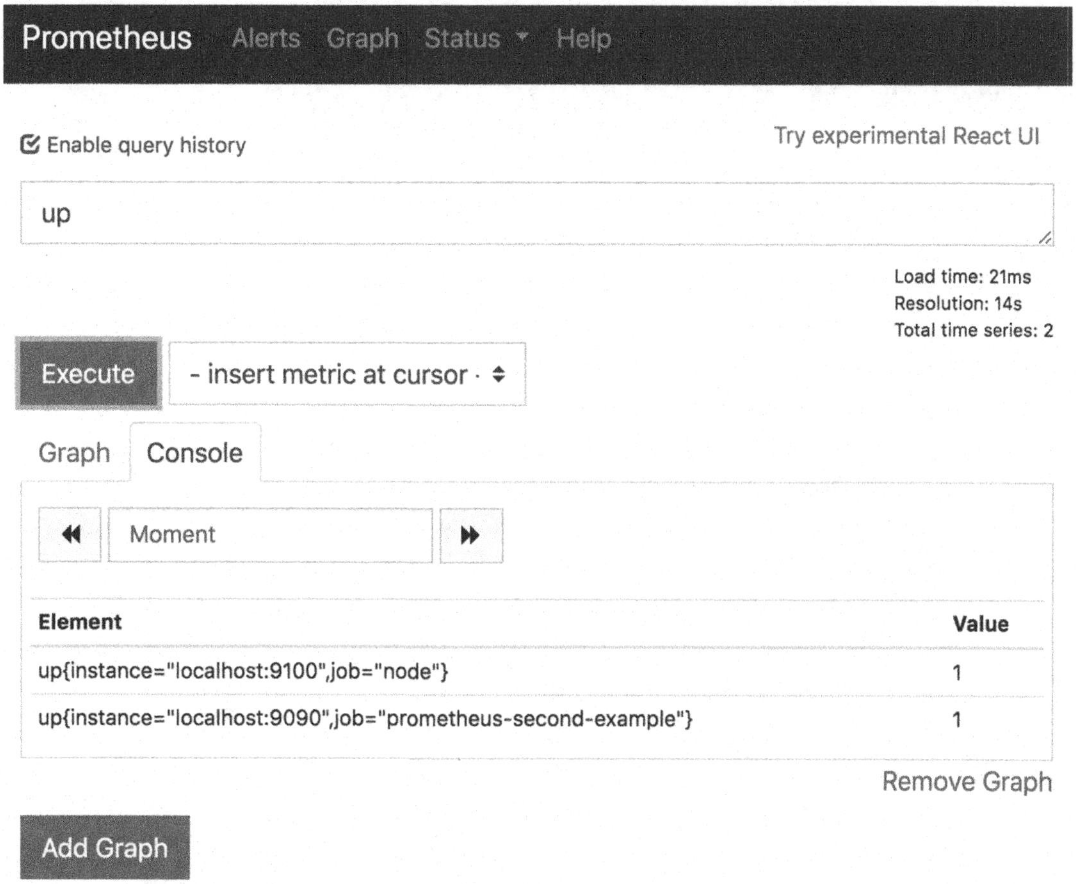

Figure 4-31. *Output of an executed query in the Console tab*

In case you are interested in the graphical representation of this expression, you can easily switch to the Graph tab, as seen in Figure 4-32, and discover two colored line graphs, each representing one specific target. You can hover on a specific line graph to check which instance that particular line graph is for. In the example in Figure 4-33, we can see that the red line corresponds to localhost:9090 (the Prometheus server) and the green line corresponds to localhost:9100 (the Node Exporter). You can see that the green line corresponding to Node Exporter went straight from 0 to 1, when the node came up and started reporting. To summarize, Graph helps you analyze the movement in the value of the time-series data collected from different targets over a period of time.

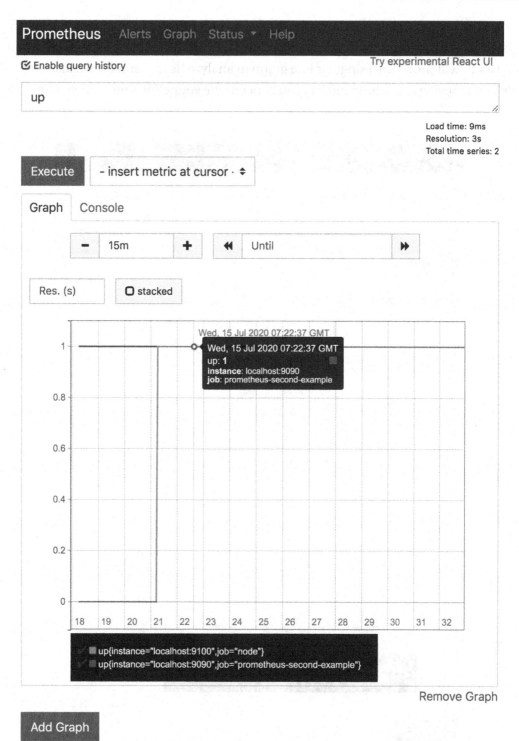

Figure 4-32. *Graphical representation*

If there are multiple targets reporting multiple line graphs and you are interested in a particular line graph to analyze its movement, you can click the particular expression and Graph will show you a singular line graph to analyze its movements exclusively. This helps in removing the clutter and lets you concentrate your efforts on a single target.

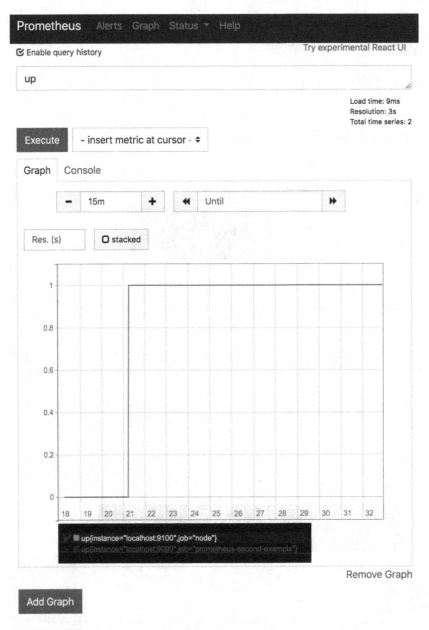

Figure 4-33. *Focusing on a single expression*

Prometheus also has an experimental UI based on React, and there is an easy link to switch from the Classic UI which we saw earlier to the React-based UI and vice versa. See Figure 4-34.

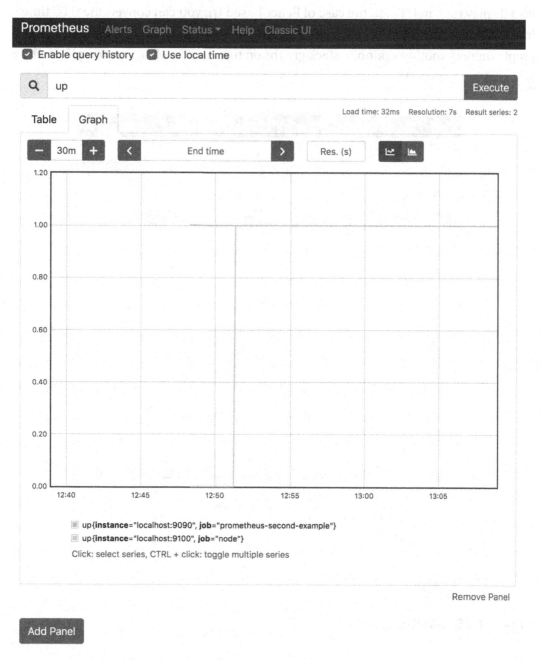

Figure 4-34. *React-based UI*

This UI is very similar to the Classic UI, apart from the difference in the look and feel and some additional features like Use Local Time. Prometheus uses UTC[3] while storing and retrieving the time-series data, and therefore all the graphs in Expression Browser also display time in UTC. In the case of React-based UI, you can convert the UTC time into local time, which makes more sense while analyzing the graph. Apart from the line graph, there is another option to stack graphs on top of each other, an example of which is shown in Figure 4-35.

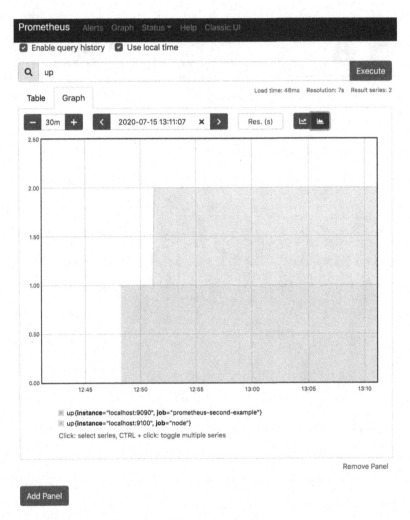

Figure 4-35. *Stacked graphs*

However, Prometheus recommends using a proper visualization platform like Grafana for creating dashboards and graphs on the time-series data coming from the Prometheus database. Grafana is a open source visualization tool, developed and managed by Grafana Labs, that has out-of-the-box support for Prometheus as a data source. We will take a detailed look at Grafana in Chapter 6 of this book.

Alerting

You can create alerting rules in Prometheus by specifying the conditions under which to fire an alert. An alert once fired can then be sent to AlertManager, which aggregates these alerts and notifies the operators through a suitable notification channel such as Email, Slack, or Pager Duty. AlertManager is a separate instance from the Prometheus server that can de-duplicate and aggregate alerts received from multiple Prometheus Servers before routing them to the relevant notification systems. Similarly, a single Prometheus server can choose to send alerts to more than one AlertManager. AlertManager, rather than just sending a one-to-one notification for each alert, does several other things, as discussed in the following:

Grouping

AlertManager can group several alerts that correspond to each other into a single notification. During an emergency, a single outage can trigger multiple subsequent outages, and each of these failed systems can fire an alert corresponding to its outage. This can easily result in an alert storm, and if each of these alerts sends a notification, as they would be configured to do so, it can result in a complete avalanche of mail notifications or pages. AlertManager can be configured to group similar alerts by logical grouping and therefore send a single notification but with the details of all the outages in the same notification.

Routing

AlertManager can be configured to send notifications to separate teams on separate notification channels in case you want to notify different teams for different kinds of alerts. For example, with a database-related issue, you would want to page the DBA and not the infrastructure admin. This can be configured using a routing tree in the configuration file, which is shown in Figure 4-36.

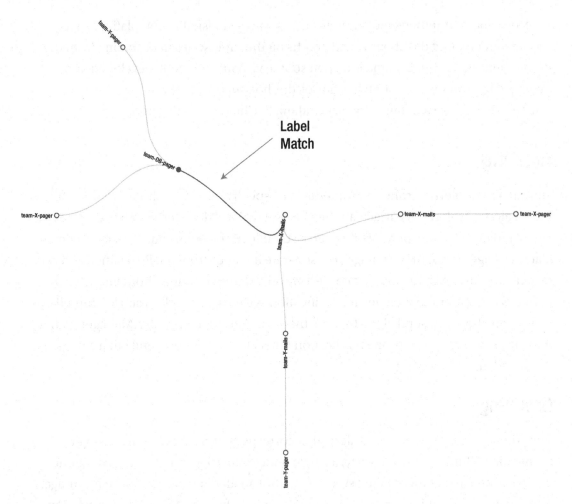

Figure 4-36. *Routing tree*

Inhibition

AlertManager can inhibit certain alerts from generating a notification, in case other alerts for a similar issue have already triggered a notification. This is useful in cases where a network issue has made a cluster inaccessible and the notification for this outage has been sent already. Now if individual systems of that cluster are also triggering their own alerts, AlertManager will inhibit them from sending notifications.

Silences

AlertManager can be configured to mute alerts for a specific duration. Silences can be configured using the user interface of the AlertManager; once activated, it will check incoming alerts on the basis of their labels. In case the labels match, notifications will not be sent until the silence is active.

CHAPTER 5

TICK Stack

TICK Stack is another popular open source time-series–based monitoring platform that was started in 2013. It is developed and maintained by InfluxData as a stack of open source software projects, namely, Telegraf (T), InfluxDB (I), Chronograf (C), and Kapacitor (K), from which it derives the name TICK Stack. TICK Stack has been recently merged into a single binary called InfluxDB 2.0, which is available both as open source software and as InfluxData supported Enterprise edition. There is a managed SaaS offering called InfluxDB also available in case the hassle of deployment and maintenance has to be avoided. For the rest of the chapter, we will use both TICK Stack and InfluxDB interchangeably, as with the new single binary, InfluxDB is the erstwhile TICK Stack.

InfluxDB is written in Go and compiles into a single binary without any external dependencies. It has a built-in HTTP API and has plug-ins for various data formats like Telegraf, Collectd, OpenTSDB, and Graphite. It also offers two SQL-like query languages, InfluxQL and Flux, to interact with the database through user interface (UI) or command-line interface (CLI).

At the heart of TICK Stack lies InfluxDB, which is a high-performance time-series datastore built to handle massive write and read loads. Since it is a time-series database, it can be used to store data points that can be either measurements spread over fixed time intervals or irregular discrete events as well. It can support ingests of millions of data points per second, which can lead to a considerable ask for storage if data is stored for longer durations. InfluxDB has an inbuilt feature to automatically compact data to minimize storage, and you can downsample the data also, keeping the high-precision current data for a smaller duration and converting the stale old data to low-precision summarized data.

InfluxDB supports high-precision data with measurements done at millisecond, microsecond, and sometimes even nanosecond intervals. This is one reason that InfluxDB is well suited for scientific or financial computing. In InfluxDB, data on the

© Mainak Chakraborty and Ajit Pratap Kundan 2021
M. Chakraborty and A. P. Kundan, *Monitoring Cloud-Native Applications*,
https://doi.org/10.1007/978-1-4842-6888-9_5

disk is organized in a columnar format with contiguous time blocks which are organized by tagset, measurement, or field. Since each field is arranged sequentially, it is faster to calculate aggregates on a single field. Also, there is no limitation on the number of tags or fields which can be used.

The common challenge for time-series databases is having limited support for multiple fields and tags and supporting only float64 values. The InfluxDB data model doesn't have such challenges, as it is specifically built to solve these issues. It supports many data formats, and fields and tags also don't have any limitation around the numbers that can be used. It lets the developer choose the schema by indexing tags and not indexing the fields.

Telegraf, the open source agent of InfluxDB, supports more than 200 plug-ins. It caters to most of the applications, systems, and network devices commonly available. It supports both pull and push mode and therefore can work in scraping or listening methods, making it a universal agent that not just supports InfluxDB but can also work with other monitoring back ends.

Installation

We can deploy InfluxDB OSS 2.0 on a Kubernetes cluster by running the InfluxDB configuration yaml[1] file. Before we go ahead and deploy InfluxDB, let's have a closer look at the yaml first in Figure 5-1:

---

[1]YAML (YAML Ain't Markup Language) is the declarative language used most commonly in cloud native environments. For more details visit www.yaml.org.

```
1  ---
2  apiVersion: v1
3  kind: Namespace
4  metadata:
5      name: influxdb
6  ---
7  apiVersion: apps/v1
8  kind: StatefulSet
9  metadata:
10     labels:
11         app: influxdb
12     name: influxdb
13     namespace: influxdb
14 spec:
15     replicas: 1
16     selector:
17         matchLabels:
18             app: influxdb
19     serviceName: influxdb
20     template:
21         metadata:
22             labels:
23                 app: influxdb
24         spec:
25             containers:
26                 - image: quay.io/influxdb/influxdb:v2.0.1
27                   name: influxdb
28                   ports:
29                     - containerPort: 8086
30                       name: influxdb
31                   volumeMounts:
32                     - mountPath: /root/.influxdbv2
33                       name: data
34     volumeClaimTemplates:
35         - metadata:
36             name: data
37             namespace: influxdb
38           spec:
39             accessModes:
40                 - ReadWriteOnce
41             resources:
```

Figure 5-1. *InfluxDB YAML configuration*

```
42                        requests:
43                            storage: 10G
44 ---
45 apiVersion: v1
46 kind: Service
47 metadata:
48     name: influxdb
49     namespace: influxdb
50 spec:
51     ports:
52       - name: influxdb
53         port: 8086
54         targetPort: 8086
55     selector:
56         app: influxdb
57     type: ClusterIP
```

Figure 5-1. *(continued)*

This yaml file has the configuration to create a separate namespace called influxdb, a separate service called influxdb, and a stateful set also called influxdb on execution. So, let's go ahead and deploy this YAML configuration using the kubectl command. Once deployed, you can check to see whether there are running pods in the namespace influxdb. If your deployment is successful, you should see the influxdb-0 pod in a running state, as shown in Figure 5-2.

```
mchakrabort-a01:~ mchakraborty$ kubectl apply -f https://raw.githubusercontent.com/influxdata/docs-v2/master/static/downloads/influxdb-k8-minikube.yaml
namespace/influxdb created
statefulset.apps/influxdb created
service/influxdb created
mchakrabort-a01:~ mchakraborty$ kubectl get pods -n influxdb
NAME         READY   STATUS    RESTARTS   AGE
influxdb-0   1/1     Running   0          31s
```

Figure 5-2. *Running InfluxDB on Kubernetes cluster*

We will run the kubectl describe command to get the endpoint IP and the associated port for the influxdb service, as shown in Figure 5-3.

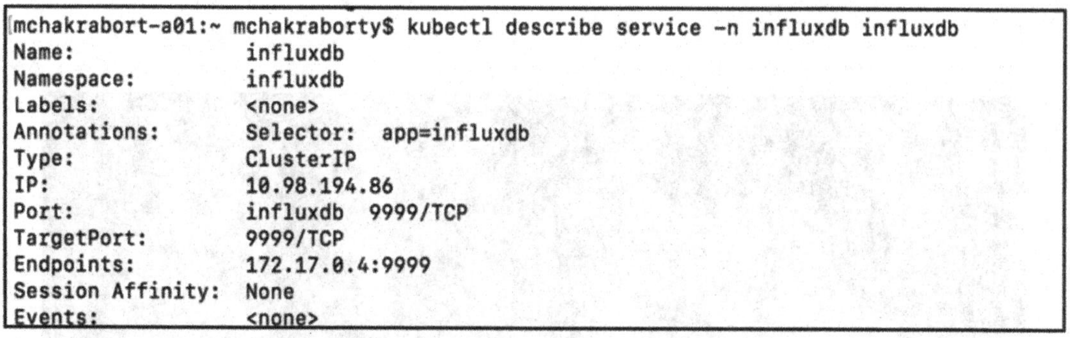

```
[mchakrabort-a01:~ mchakraborty$ kubectl describe service -n influxdb influxdb
Name:                influxdb
Namespace:           influxdb
Labels:              <none>
Annotations:         Selector:   app=influxdb
Type:                ClusterIP
IP:                  10.98.194.86
Port:                influxdb   9999/TCP
TargetPort:          9999/TCP
Endpoints:           172.17.0.4:9999
Session Affinity:    None
Events:              <none>
```

Figure 5-3. *Describing the InfluxDB pod*

Once we have these details, we can run the kubectl port-forward command to forward port 9999 from inside the cluster to localhost, as seen in Figure 5-4.

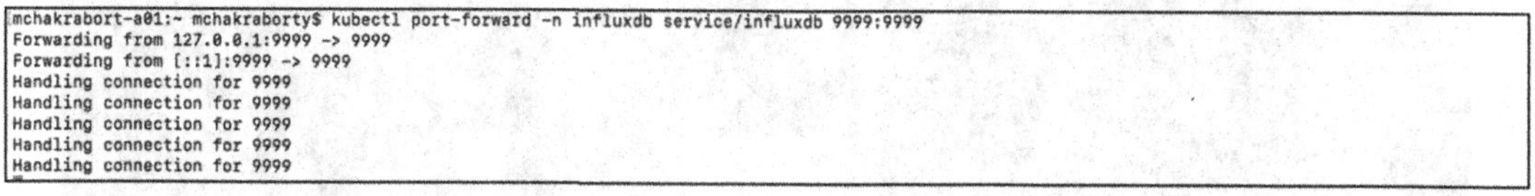

```
mchakrabort-a01:~ mchakraborty$ kubectl port-forward -n influxdb service/influxdb 9999:9999
Forwarding from 127.0.0.1:9999 -> 9999
Forwarding from [::1]:9999 -> 9999
Handling connection for 9999
Handling connection for 9999
Handling connection for 9999
Handling connection for 9999
Handling connection for 9999
```

Figure 5-4. *Port forwarding on localhost*

If the installation happened successfully, InfluxDB UI should be accessible at http://localhost:9999/ (see Figure 5-5).

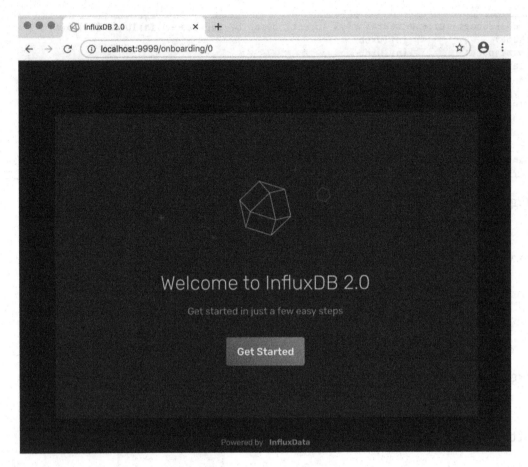

Figure 5-5. *Welcome screen for successful installation*

During the setup process for InfluxDB, you have to provide a username and a password. It also requires you to create a default organization and a bucket. The setup process is available in both the InfluxDB UI and the influx CLI. See Figure 5-6.

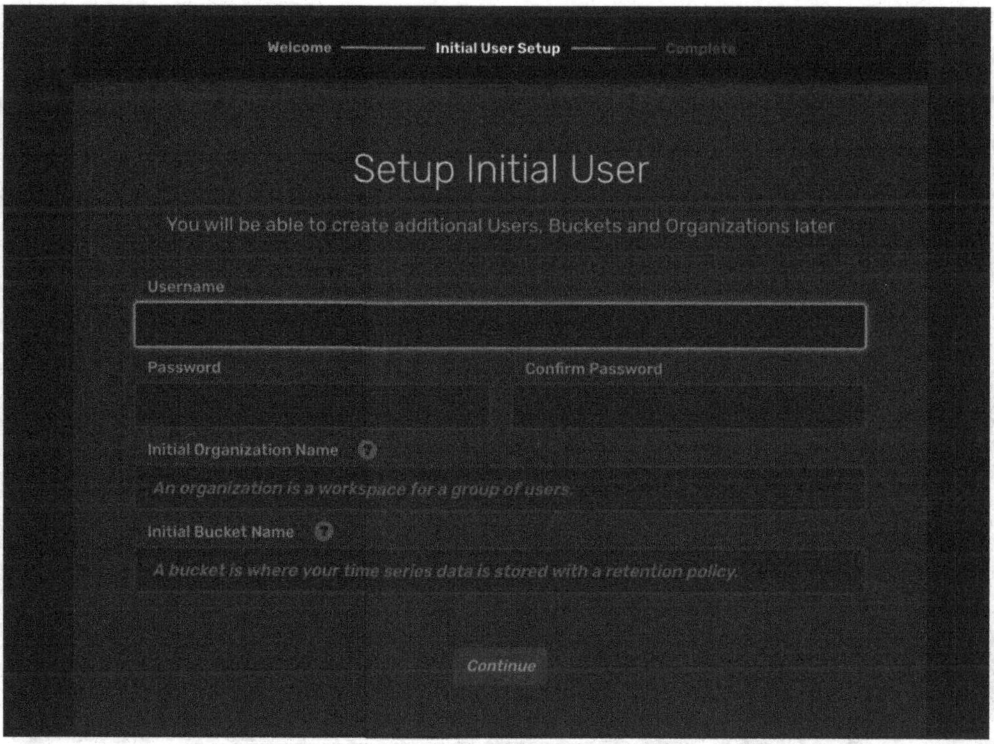

Figure 5-6. *Initial setup screen*

Once filled, this will look similar to Figure 5-7. Click Continue to move to the next page:

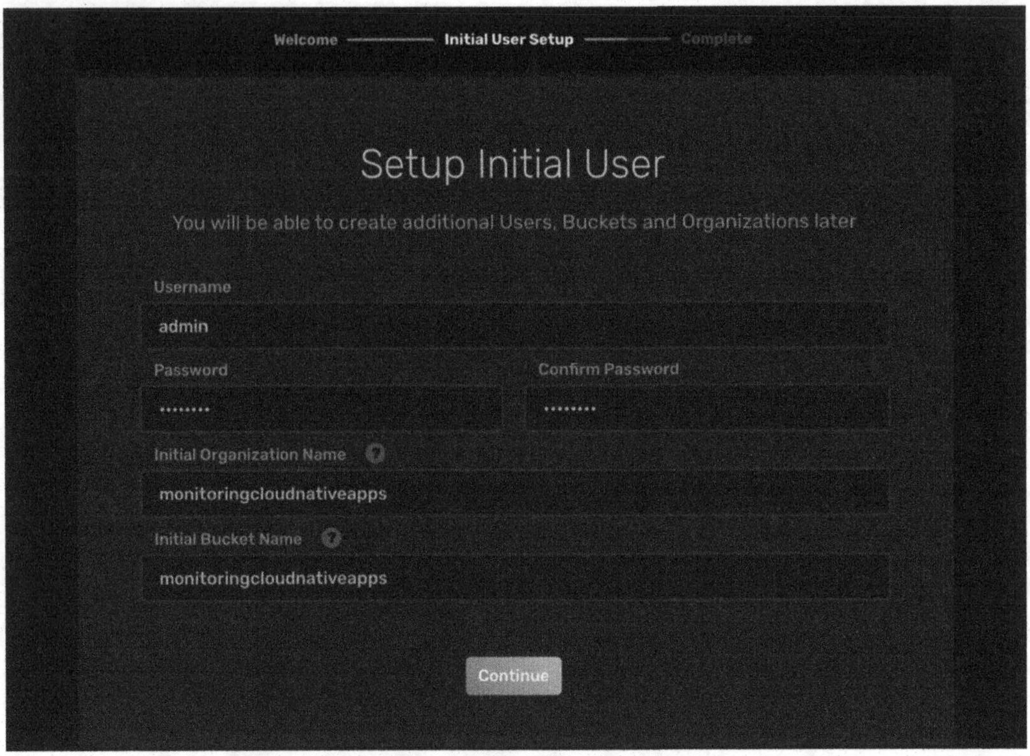

Figure 5-7. *Setup screen with all the fields populated*

Once the setup is complete, you will be greeted with the landing page for InfluxDB, as shown in Figure 5-8:

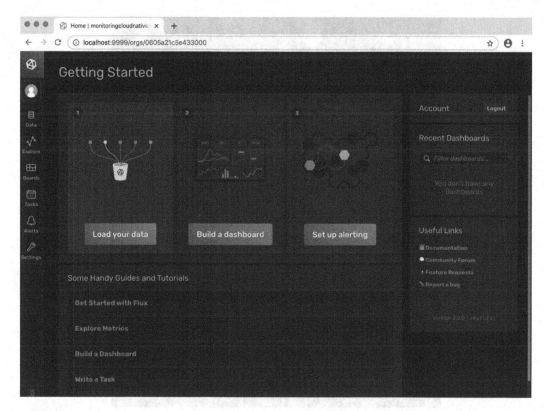

Figure 5-8. *Landing page for InfluxDB*

At this stage, it is prudent to log out and use the username and password from the Setup screen to log in again, as shown in Figure 5-9.

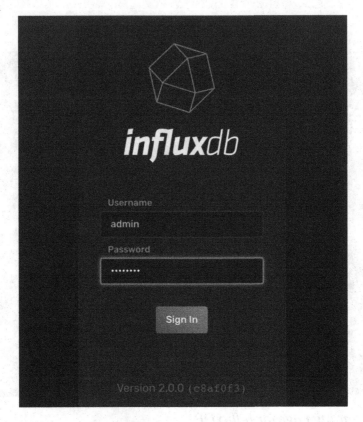

Figure 5-9. *Login screen of InfluxDB*

Key Concepts in InfluxDB

Organization

Organization is a logical workspace inside InfluxDB that can contain buckets, dashboards, and tasks. A set of users belong to an organization, and each user is associated with a particular role. In Figure 5-10, the current organization is set to *monitoringcloudnativeapps*. Every organization is associated with an organization ID.

Creating an Organization

You can create a new organization using the UI by selecting Create Organization[2] from the drop-down, as shown in Figure 5-10. This will open up a Create Organization window, where you can provide a unique organization name along with a bucket name.

---

[2]Not available with InfluxDB Cloud

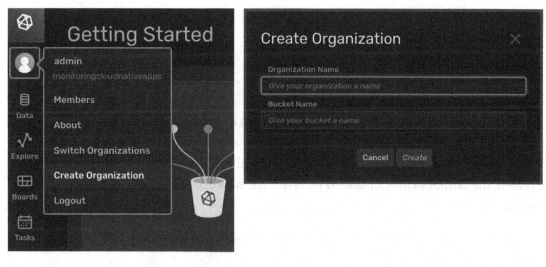

Figure 5-10. *Create organization through UI*

After configuring more than one organization, it is easy to switch from one organization to another using the Switch Organizations option from the drop-down and selecting the option which you want to set as the current organization. In Figure 5-11, the current organization is set as *monitoringcloudnativeapps,* which can be switched to another organization by selecting *monitoringcloudnativeapps2* if so desired.

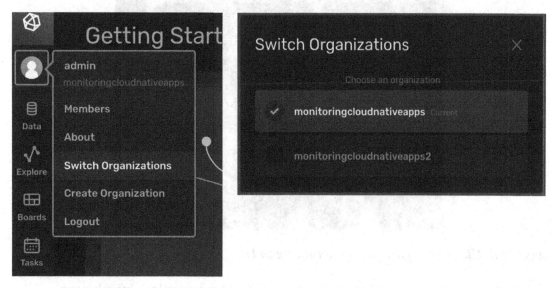

Figure 5-11. *Switch organizations through UI*

143

It is easy to do the same thing via CLI using Influx CLI and the *influx org create* command. The syntax of the command is

```
$ influx org create --host <http://hostname:port> --token <INFLUX_TOKEN>
--name <org name>
```

An implementation of this command is shown in Figure 5-12. Note to pass the **Admin token** in the <INFLUX_TOKEN> section from the tokens available under the Load Data section (explained later in the "Data Collection" section). Once successfully created, the output of the command will have the new org name and the associated ID with it.

```
mchakrabort-a01:~ mchakraborty$ influx org create --host http://localhost:9999 --token xjyAcEZusDQWjbneCGsyu2QV260XLTMVRMgGkhAd1
Z1Ns1OQqW-Rxc7gP0oe6cJ_eLWHSbMruzLAunXcgoLQoA== --name monitoringcloudnativeapps3
ID                      Name
0607f632bb433000        monitoringcloudnativeapps3
```

Figure 5-12. *Create organization using CLI*

To confirm whether the new organization is created, check the UI under the Switch Organizations section. Your new org name should show up in the list, as shown in Figure 5-13.

Figure 5-13. *New organization available in UI*

You can also use the CLI in order to view the list of organizations by using the following command:

```
$ influx org list --host <http://hostname:port> --token <INFLUX_TOKEN>
```

The output of the command will look like Figure 5-14 with a list of organizations and their respective IDs:

```
mchakrabort-a01:~ mchakraborty$ influx org list --host http://localhost:9999 --token xjyAcEZusDQWjbneCGsyu2QV260XLTMVRMgGkhA
dlZlNs1OQqW-Rxc7gP0oe6cJ_eLWHSbMruzLAunXcgoLQoA==
ID                    Name
0605a21c5e433000      monitoringcloudnativeapps
06075092bfc33000      monitoringcloudnativeapps2
0607f632bb433000      monitoringcloudnativeapps3
```

Figure 5-14. *View organization using CLI*

Renaming an Organization

When you need to rename an existing organization name to something more meaningful, you can use the About section from the drop-down menu, which leads to the Organization tab, as shown in Figure 5-15.

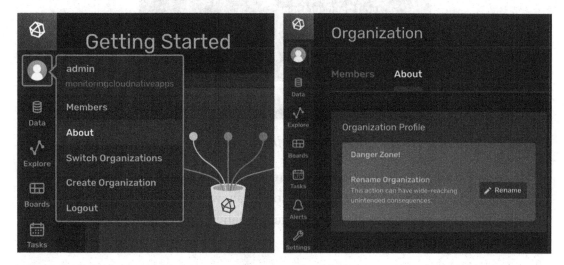

Figure 5-15. *Rename an organization using UI*

Click Rename and it will pop up a disclaimer citing a concern that any name change will lead to associated queries, dashboards, tasks, and other configurations that won't be working as expected, as they will still be referencing the old organization name. Make sure to update these soon after modifying the organization name so that earlier configurations work seamlessly. See Figure 5-16.

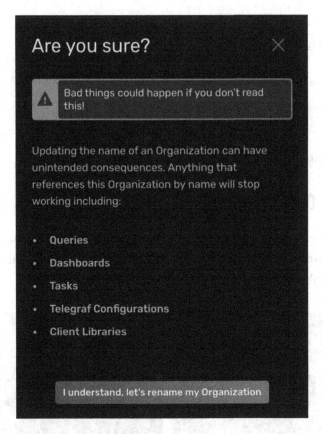

Figure 5-16. *Things to note before renaming*

Once you move ahead accepting that there can be consequences for the organization name change, you can rename the organization, as shown in Figure 5-17, where the current organization name of monitoringcloudnativeapps3 is being modified to monitoringcloudnativeapps4.

Figure 5-17. *Renaming an organization through UI*

Once the organization name has been successfully modified, it will appear in the Switch Organizations section, as shown in Figure 5-18:

Figure 5-18. *Renames organization in the list of organizations*

This can be achieved easily thorugh the CLI using the following command:

```
$ influx org update --host <http://hostname:port> --token <INFLUX_TOKEN>
-i<org-id> -n <new-org-name>
```

The output of the command will look like the highlighted section in Figure 5-19 and will provide the revised organization name with the existing org-id:

```
mchakrabort-a01:~ mchakraborty$ influx org list --host http://localhost:9999 --token xjyAcEZusDQWjbneCGsyu2QV260XLTMVRMgGkhAdlZ1Ns1OQqW-Rxc7gP0oe6cJ_eLWHSbMruzLAunXcgoLQoA
==
ID                      Name
0605a21c5e433000        monitoringcloudnativeapps
06075092bfc33000        monitoringcloudnativeapps2
0607f632bb433000        monitoringcloudnativeapps4
mchakrabort-a01:~ mchakraborty$ influx org update --host http://localhost:9999 --token xjyAcEZusDQWjbneCGsyu2QV260XLTMVRMgGkhAdlZ1Ns1OQqW-Rxc7gP0oe6cJ_eLWHSbMruzLAunXcgoLQ
oA== -i 0607f632bb433000 -n monitoringcloudnativeapps3
ID                      Name
0607f632bb433000        monitoringcloudnativeapps3
mchakrabort-a01:~ mchakraborty$ influx org list --host http://localhost:9999 --token xjyAcEZusDQWjbneCGsyu2QV260XLTMVRMgGkhAdlZ1Ns1OQqW-Rxc7gP0oe6cJ_eLWHSbMruzLAunXcgoLQoA
==
ID                      Name
0605a21c5e433000        monitoringcloudnativeapps
06075092bfc33000        monitoringcloudnativeapps2
0607f632bb433000        monitoringcloudnativeapps3
```

Figure 5-19. *Renaming an organization with CLI*

Deleting an Organization

There is no option to delete an organization using the UI[3] and therefore the only option is to use CLI. The syntax for the command to achieve this function is mentioned in the following:

```
$ influx org delete --host <http://hostname:port> --token <INFLUX_TOKEN>
-i<org-id>
```

The output of the command will look like the highlighted section in Figure 5-20 and will provide the revised organization name with the existing org-id:

```
mchakrabort-a01:~ mchakraborty$ influx org delete --host http://localhost:9999 --token xjyAcEZusDQWjbneCGsyu2QV260XLTMVRMgGk
hAd1Z1Ns10QqW-Rxc7gP0oe6cJ_eLWHSbMruzLAunXcgoLQoA== -i 0607f632bb433000
ID                      Name                    Deleted
0607f632bb433000        monitoringcloudnativeapps3      true
mchakrabort-a01:~ mchakraborty$ influx org list --host http://localhost:9999 --token xjyAcEZusDQWjbneCGsyu2QV260XLTMVRMgGkhA
d1Z1Ns10QqW-Rxc7gP0oe6cJ_eLWHSbMruzLAunXcgoLQoA==
ID                      Name
0605a21c5e433000        monitoringcloudnativeapps
06075092bfc33000        monitoringcloudnativeapps2
```

Figure 5-20. *Deleting an organization through CLI*

Members

In InfluxDB, there is a concept of a user and a member. Users are the individuals with access to InfluxDB, and when these users are part of one or more organizations, they are referred to as the members of that organization. You can get a list of users and their user IDs by using the CLI to run the following syntax:

```
$ influx user list --host <http://hostname:port> --token <INFLUX_TOKEN>
```

When you run this command, you will get the username and associated user ID. In this case, since we haven't created any new users yet, it will list only the admin user. See Figure 5-21.

```
mchakrabort-a01:~ mchakraborty$ influx user list --host http://localhost:9999 --token xjyAcEZusDQWjbneCGsyu2QV260XLTMVRMgGkh
Ad1Z1Ns10QqW-Rxc7gP0oe6cJ_eLWHSbMruzLAunXcgoLQoA==
ID                      Name
0605a21c4c433000        admin
```

Figure 5-21. *List of users through CLI*

---

[3]Not available with InfluxDB Cloud

You can check the same thing in the UI from the About section in the organization page. In Figure 5-22, you can see that the user ID for an admin remains same across different organizations. For example, admin has a user ID of 0605a21c4c433000, which remains the same even when the organization changes from 0605a21c4c433000 to 06075092bfc33000.

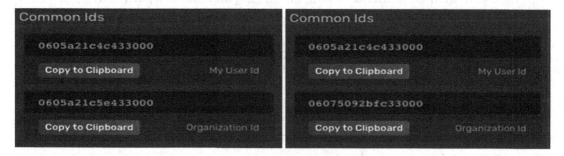

Figure 5-22. *My user ID and organization ID*

Creating a New User

You can use the *influx user create* command to create a new user with its username and password.

```
$ influx user create-n <username> -p <password> -o <org name> --token
<INFLUX_TOKEN>
```

When you run this command, you create a new user with the specified username and password. You can also run the *influx user list* command we learned about earlier to list the number of total users in InfluxDB. Notice that the user mainak is associated with the organization monitoringcloudnativeapps; therefore, mainak is a member of that particular organization. See Figure 5-23.

```
mchakrabort-a01:~ mchakraborty$ influx user create -n mainak -p password -o monitoringcloudnativeapps --token
xjyAcEZusDQWjbneCGsyu2QV260XLTMVRMgGkhAd1Z1Ns1OQqW-Rxc7gP0oe6cJ_eLWHSbMruzLAunXcgoLQoA==
ID                 Name
060998d2b6c33000   mainak
mchakrabort-a01:~ mchakraborty$ influx user list --host http://localhost:9999 --token xjyAcEZusDQWjbneCGsyu2QV
260XLTMVRMgGkhAd1Z1Ns1OQqW-Rxc7gP0oe6cJ_eLWHSbMruzLAunXcgoLQoA==
ID                 Name
0605a21c4c433000   admin
060998d2b6c33000   mainak
```

Figure 5-23. *Creating a user through CLI*

Now let's try and add the user mainak to the second organization, monitoringcloudnativeapps2, through CLI by using the *influx org members add* command, as shown in the following:

```
$ influx org members add -n <org name> -m <user id> --token <INFLUX_TOKEN>
```

When you run this command, it adds an existing member of a particular organization to a different organization as well, as shown in Figure 5-24:

```
mchakrabort-a01:~ mchakraborty$ influx user list --host http://localhost:9999 --token xjyAcEZusDQWjbneCGs
yu2QV260XLTMVRMgGkhAdlZlNs10QqW-Rxc7gP0oe6cJ_eLWHSbMruzLAunXcgoLQoA==
ID                      Name
[0605a21c4c433000       admin
060998d2b6c33000        mainak
mchakrabort-a01:~ mchakraborty$ influx org members add -n monitoringcloudnativeapps2 -m 060998d2b6c33000
[--token xjyAcEZusDQWjbneCGsyu2QV260XLTMVRMgGkhAdlZlNs10QqW-Rxc7gP0oe6cJ_eLWHSbMruzLAunXcgoLQoA==
user 060998d2b6c33000 has been added as a member of orgs: 06075092bfc33000
```

Figure 5-24. *Adding a member to an org*

You can also verify by running the *influx org members list* command as per the mentioned syntax:

```
$ influx org members list-n <org name> --token <INFLUX_TOKEN>
```

The output of the command looks like Figure 5-25. The command will provide a list of members with their user IDs, user type, and status.

```
[mchakrabort-a01:~ mchakraborty$ influx org members list -n monitoringcloudnativeapps --token xjyAcEZusDQW]
jbneCGsyu2QV260XLTMVRMgGkhAdlZlNs10QqW-Rxc7gP0oe6cJ_eLWHSbMruzLAunXcgoLQoA==
ID                      Name    User Type       Status
060998d2b6c33000        <nil>   member          active
```

Figure 5-25. *List of members in org monitoringcloudnativeapps*

Let's run the same command to check if user mainak shows up in the member's list of the second organization or not. Viola! It does, as you can see in Figure 5-26.

```
[mchakrabort-a01:~ mchakraborty$ influx org members list -n monitoringcloudnativeapps2 --token xjyAcEZusDQ]
WjbneCGsyu2QV260XLTMVRMgGkhAdlZlNs10QqW-Rxc7gP0oe6cJ_eLWHSbMruzLAunXcgoLQoA==
ID                      Name    User Type       Status
060998d2b6c33000        <nil>   member          active
```

Figure 5-26. *List of members in org monitoringcloudnativeapps2*

Updating a Username

You can update the username of an existing user by running the *influx user update* command[4]:

```
$ influx user update -i<user id> -n <new user name> --token <INFLUX_TOKEN>
```

When you run this command in the CLI, you can see the user ID being replaced by a new username, as in Figure 5-27.

```
mchakraborty-a01:~ mchakraborty$ influx user update -i 060998d2b6c33000 -n peter --token xjyAcEZusDQWjbneCGsyu2QV260XLTMVRMgGkhAdlZ1Ns1OQqW-Rxc7gP0be6cJ_eLWHSbMruzLAunXcgoL
QoA==
ID                      Name
060998d2b6c33000        peter
```

Figure 5-27. *Updating username in an organization through CLI*

The change in the username also shows up in the influx UI, as seen in Figure 5-28.

Figure 5-28. *Updated username in an organization*

---

[4]User information cannot be updated in the InfluxDB UI.

Removing a Member

You can remove a member from an organization either by deleting the member from the UI or by removing using the CLI. When you remove a member from an organization, it doesn't delete the user from InfluxDB; it only revokes the association of the member with the organization and all the permissions it had. You can use the *influx org members remove* command as per the syntax in the following:

```
$ influx org members remove -m <member id > -i<org id> --token
<INFLUX_TOKEN>
```

When you run this command in the CLI, you can see that the specific user ID being removed from the members list, as depicted in Figure 5-29.

```
[mchakrabort-a01:~ mchakraborty$ influx org members list -n monitoringcloudnativeapps2 --token xjyAcEZusDQWjbneCGsyu2]
QV26OXLTMVRMgGkhAdlZ1Ns1OQqW-Rxc7gP0oe6cJ_eLWHSbMruzLAunXcgoLQoA==
ID               Name        User Type     Status
060998d2b6c33000        <nil>   member        active
[mchakrabort-a01:~ mchakraborty$ influx org list --host http://localhost:9999 --token xjyAcEZusDQWjbneCGsyu2QV26OXLTM]
VRMgGkhAdlZ1Ns1OQqW-Rxc7gP0oe6cJ_eLWHSbMruzLAunXcgoLQoA==
ID               Name
0605a21c5e433000        monitoringcloudnativeapps
06075092bfc33000        monitoringcloudnativeapps2
[mchakrabort-a01:~ mchakraborty$ influx org members remove -m 060998d2b6c33000 -i 06075092bfc33000 --token xjyAcEZusD]
QWjbneCGsyu2QV26OXLTMVRMgGkhAdlZ1Ns1OQqW-Rxc7gP0oe6cJ_eLWHSbMruzLAunXcgoLQoA==
userID 060998d2b6c33000 has been removed from ResourceID 06075092bfc33000
[mchakrabort-a01:~ mchakraborty$ influx org members list -n monitoringcloudnativeapps2 --token xjyAcEZusDQWjbneCGsyu2]
QV26OXLTMVRMgGkhAdlZ1Ns1OQqW-Rxc7gP0oe6cJ_eLWHSbMruzLAunXcgoLQoA==
ID        Name     User Type       Status
mchakrabort-a01:~ mchakraborty$ █
```

Figure 5-29. *Removing a member from an organization through CLI*

The same thing can be achieved using UI by removing the user peter, who is a member of the organization monitoringcloudnativeapps2, by clicking the trash can, as shown in Figure 5-30.

Figure 5-30. *Removing a member from an organization through UI*

Deleting a User

A user can be permanently deleted by using the *influx user delete* command through the CLI as per the following syntax[5]:

```
$ influx user delete -i<User id> --token <INFLUX_TOKEN>
```

Once executed, it will delete the user named peter, as depicted in Figure 5-31:

```
[mchakrabort-a01:~ mchakraborty$ influx user list --token xjyAcEZusDQWjbneCGsyu2QV260XLTMVRMgGkhAdlZlNs1OQqW-Rxc7gP0o]
e6cJ_eLWHSbMruzLAunXcgoLQoA==
ID                      Name
0605a21c4c433000        admin
060998d2b6c33000        peter
[mchakrabort-a01:~ mchakraborty$ influx user delete -i 060998d2b6c33000 --token xjyAcEZusDQWjbneCGsyu2QV260XLTMVRMgGk]
hAdlZlNs1OQqW-Rxc7gP0oe6cJ_eLWHSbMruzLAunXcgoLQoA==
ID                      Name    Deleted
060998d2b6c33000        peter   true
```

Figure 5-31. *Removing a user from InfluxDB through CLI*

---

[5]Users cannot be deleted from the InfluxDB UI.

Buckets

A bucket is associated with an organization and stores all the time-series data. Buckets have a retention policy to store data points only for a particular time period as dictated by the retention policy.

You can use the UI to *Create Bucket* from two different places: one from the **Load Data - Buckets** page as shown in Figure 5-32 and the second from the **Data Explorer - From** page.

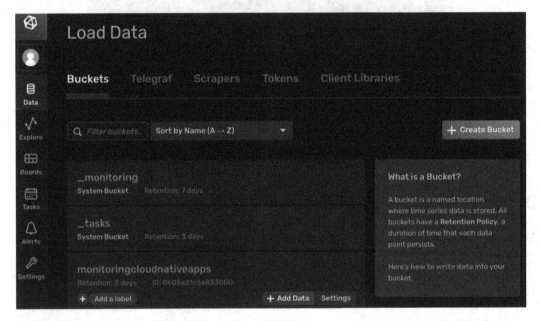

Figure 5-32. *Create bucket from Load Data*

Data Collection

Scraper

In order to write data into InfluxDB, you need to configure first the organization, then the bucket and also the authentication token. We have seen how to set these up in the "Installation" section and their meaning in the "Key Concepts in InfluxDB" section. Now, to quickly get started, you can create a Scraper that scrapes data from any HTTP/S-accessible endpoint providing data in the Prometheus data format at regular time intervals and then writes them to a bucket to store all the data. We will configure the Scraper to scrape metrics from InfluxDB itself using the target endpoint as `http://localhost:9999/metrics`. These internal metrics serve as a good dataset to get started on how to get data and visualize it in InfluxDB. See Figure 5-33.

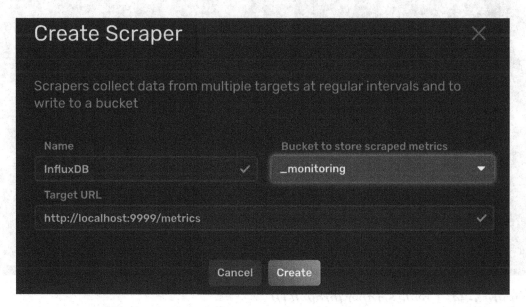

Figure 5-33. *Create Scraper through UI*

Once Scraper is configured, you can see the metrics data that it is collecting at the Data Explorer _monitoring bucket and filter out the fields that you want to concentrate on, as shown in Figure 5-34:

Figure 5-34. *Create Scraper through UI*

Similar to this, you can create Scraper for applications and tools that generate metrics in the Prometheus data format and ingest those in InfluxDB for further processing and visualization.

Telegraf

The data collection agent for Influx platform is Telegraf. It has a vast number of 200+ plug-ins that allow it to collect metrics easily from almost any source. Telegraf consists of input plug-ins and output plug-ins configured in telegraf.conf, which is the configuration file for Telegraf. In this section, we will learn how to install Telegraf, configure it, and write metrics into InfluxDB.

Telegraf Installation

Based on the choice of Telegraf plug-in selected, the InfluxDB UI can create the telegraf. conf file. Since only a few plug-ins are configurable through the InfluxDB UI, for the rest of the plug-ins we would have to manually configure the telegraf.conf file.

To start creating the Telegraf configuration, you need to come to the Create Configuration page in Load Data - Telegraf section. You can see in Figure 5-35 that there are no configurations created as yet.

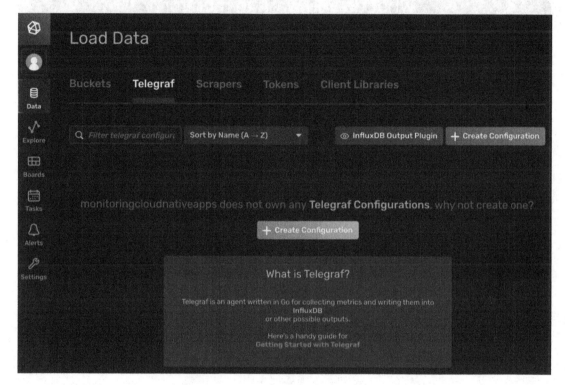

Figure 5-35. *Telegraf configuration using UI*

Click Create Configuration. In the next page that opens up, you are presented with a choice of selecting the Telegraf plug-in which you want to configure. Notice that plug-ins are only available for System, Docker, Kubernetes, NGINX, and Redis to be configured through the UI. Let's first select a bucket from the drop-down menu and try to configure the system plug-in, as shown in Figure 5-36.

Figure 5-36. Creating a Telegraf configuration for System[6]

After providing a name and description for the configuration, press **Create and Verify,** as shown in Figure 5-37:

---

[6]For this setup, the system considered is MacOS.

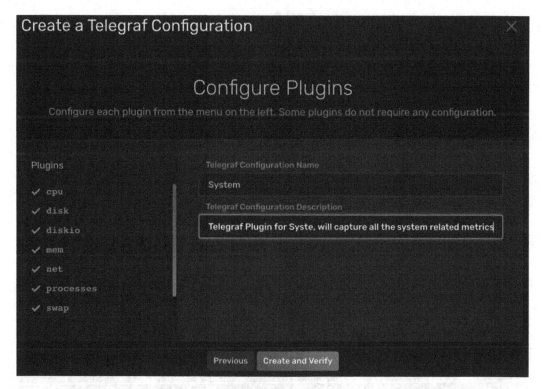

Figure 5-37. *Configuring TelegrafSystem plug-in*

The next step is to install Telegraf agent as per the instructions in Figure 5-38.

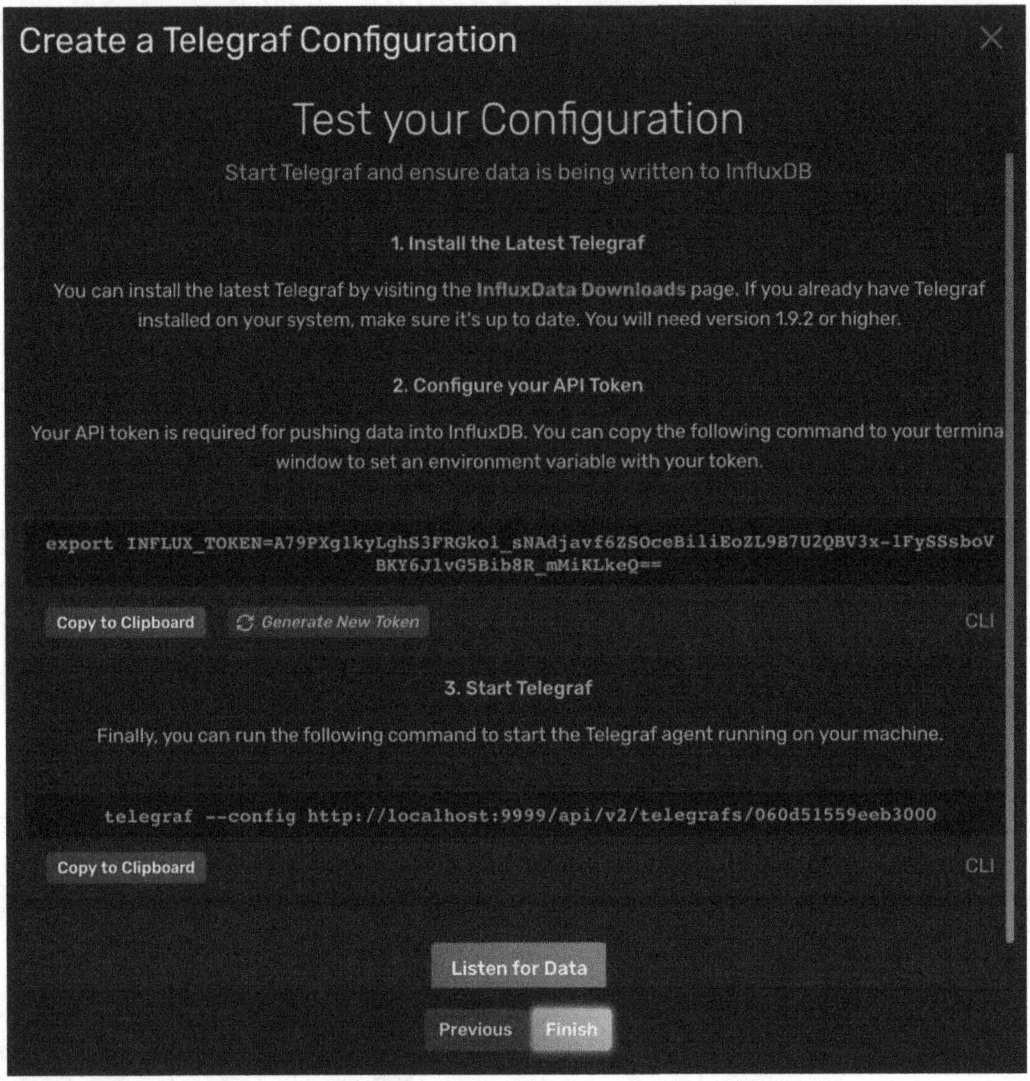

Figure 5-38. *Telegraf installation*

Once Telegraf is installed, configure Telegraf to interact with the InfluxDB setup, which is running using the commands from Step 2 and Step 3, executed as shown in the command prompt in Figure 5-39.[7]

Figure 5-39. *Setting up Telegraf to interact with InfluxDB*

Click **Listen for Data** in UI, as shown in Figure 5-38. If everything is successfully configured, you will get a **Connection Found!** confirmation, as shown in Figure 5-40:

```
                        Connection Found!

        monitoringcloudnativeapps is receiving data loud and clear!
```

Figure 5-40. *Successful connection set up between Telegraf and InfluxDB for System plug-in*

Let's check the **Data Explorer** page for the metrics that Telegraf plugged in for System should be ingesting into InfluxDB. If you check in the bucket monitoringcloudnativeapps, you should see some metrics pertaining to cpu, disk, diskio, mem, and so forth. You can choose filters as required, and once you hit **Submit,** you should be able to visualize graphs such as the one shown in Figure 5-41.

---

[7]I have used a separate token for authentication in Figure 5-40. You should enter the one displayed in UI.

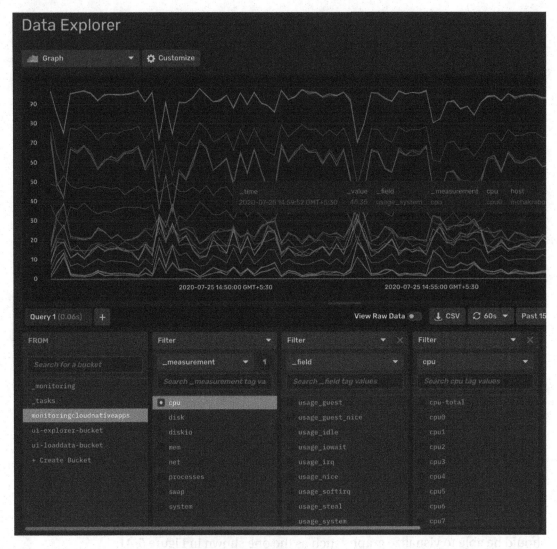

Figure 5-41. *Graphical representation of the data collected through Telegraf plug-in for System*

Manual Telegraf Configuration

In case you want to gather inputs from environments other than the ones shown in the plug-in UI, there is a way of manually configuring the Telegraf configuration file (telegraf. conf) to capture data from multiple input sources and send the data to InfluxDB. This is done by configuring the telegraf.conf file to include an input plug-in that collects metrics in conjunction with the influxdb_v2 output plug-in that writes metrics into InfluxDB bucket. Let's see an example to get more understanding.

1. First, we need to find an input plug-in we are interested in from the Telegraf plug-ins page, accessible at `https://v2.docs.influxdata.com/v2.0/reference/telegraf-plugins/`. There is a wide variety of plug-ins available to collect metrics from applications and third-party systems and use with InfluxDB. For Figure 5-42, we have selected OpenWeatherMap as our input plug-in.

Figure 5-42. *OpenWeatherMap input plug-in*

2. Clicking View will open the Telegraf input plug-ins page on GitHub. You can read through what the plug-in does and copy and paste the configuration into your telegraf.conf file.

3. InfluxDB output configuration is available at the Load Data - Telegraf page. Download the config and paste in the telegraf.conf to send data to an InfluxDB v2.0 instance, as shown in Figure 5-43.

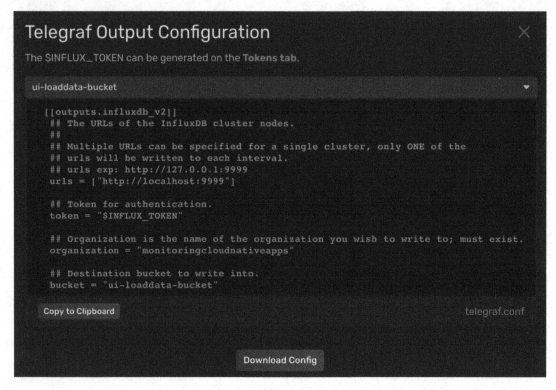

Figure 5-43. *InfluxDB output plug-in*

Figure 5-44 shows how the telegraf.conf file should look after including both plug-ins:

```
1   [[inputs.openweathermap]]
2     ## OpenWeatherMap API key.
3     app_id = "replace with API key"
4
5     ## City ID's to collect weather data from.
6     city_id = ["5391959"]
7
8     ## Language of the description field. Can be one of "ar", "bg",
9     ## "ca", "cz", "de", "el", "en", "fa", "fi", "fr", "gl", "hr", "hu",
10    ## "it", "ja", "kr", "la", "lt", "mk", "nl", "pl", "pt", "ro", "ru",
11    ## "se", "sk", "sl", "es", "tr", "ua", "vi", "zh_cn", "zh_tw",
12    # lang = "en"
13
14    ## APIs to fetch; can contain "weather" or "forecast".
15    fetch = ["weather", "forecast"]
16
17    ## OpenWeatherMap base URL
18    # base_url = "https://api.openweathermap.org/"
19
20    ## Timeout for HTTP response.
21    # response_timeout = "5s"
22
23    ## Preferred unit system for temperature and wind speed. Can be one of
24    ## "metric", "imperial", or "standard".
25    # units = "metric"
26
27    ## Query interval; OpenWeatherMap weather data is updated every 10
28    ## minutes.
29    interval = "10m"
30    [[outputs.influxdb_v2]]
31    ## The URLs of the InfluxDB cluster nodes.
32    ##
33    ## Multiple URLs can be specified for a single cluster, only ONE of the
34    ## urls will be written to each interval.
35    ## urls exp: http://127.0.0.1:9999
36    urls = ["http://localhost:9999"]
37
38    ## Token for authentication.
39    token = "$INFLUX_TOKEN"
40
41    ## Organization is the name of the organization you wish to write to; must exist.
42    organization = "monitoringcloudnativeapps"
43
44    ## Destination bucket to write into.
45    bucket = "ui-loaddata-bucket"
46
```

Figure 5-44. *telegraf.conf file with both plug-ins included*

Use the --config flag to provide the path to telegraf.conf file and start the telegraf service.

```
$ telegraf --config /path/to/custom/telegraf.conf
```

Once the command is executed, the output will look like the screenshot in Figure 5-45.

```
mchakrabort-a01:Tick_Stack mchakraborty$ telegraf --config telegraf.conf
2020-07-25T13:16:28Z I! Starting Telegraf 1.14.5
2020-07-25T13:16:28Z I! Loaded inputs: openweathermap
2020-07-25T13:16:28Z I! Loaded aggregators:
2020-07-25T13:16:28Z I! Loaded processors:
2020-07-25T13:16:28Z I! Loaded outputs: influxdb_v2
2020-07-25T13:16:28Z I! Tags enabled: host=mchakrabort-a01.vmware.com
2020-07-25T13:16:28Z I! [agent] Config: Interval:10s, Quiet:false, Hostname:"mchakrabort-a01.vmware.com", Flush Interval:10s
```

Figure 5-45. *Telegraf service started*

Now you should be able to visualize the output of this plug-in in the **Data Explorer** in the configured bucket, in this case, **ui-loaddata-bucket.** You need to select the bucket and the respective filters, select the time period of collection, and click Submit. You should be able to see line graphs, as shown in Figure 5-46:

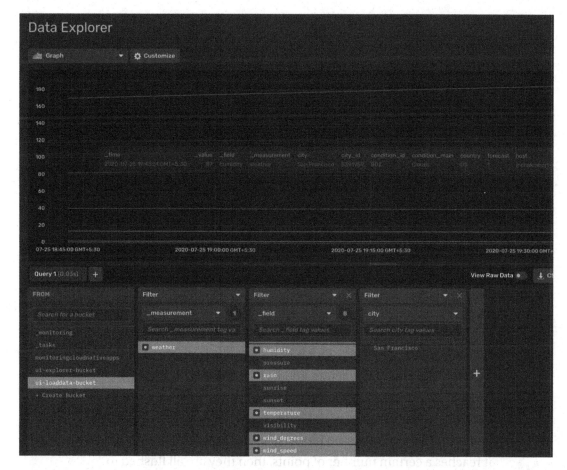

Figure 5-46. *Line graph depicting data from OpenWeatherMapTelegraf plug-in*

This plug-in provides weather data including humidity, rain, temperature, wind speed, and wind direction for the city of San Francisco. This section demonstrates how easy it is to configure InfluxDB to receive data not only for IT systems but for just about any kind of time series.

Data Storage

InfluxDB is based on SSTables from the concept of LSM-Tree[8] in LevelDB, which was actually used as a storage engine in the earlier versions of InfluxDB. InfluxDB's own storage engine, which is based on Time-Structured-Merge (TSM) Tree, is a collection

---

[8]LSM-Tree is explained in detail in Chapter 3.

of different components including the external interface which is used for writing and querying time-series data.

InfluxDB storage engine has a write-ahead log (WAL) where writes are stored before they are persisted thus providing write durability in the case of a sudden restart. It also has read only data files called as TSM files that contain compressed time-series data in a sorted columnar format. A TSM file is very similar to an LSM file. The storage engine uses WAL to write an optimized storage format and map the index files to memory.

InfluxDB creates shard for a time block from the entire duration under consideration. For example, if the retention policy is for 1 month, then shards for a 7-day time period can be created and mapped to a database in the underlying storage. Each of these individual databases would have their own WAL and TSM files.

> **In-memory index**: It is a shared index across shards which provides quick access to measurement, tags, and series.
>
> **WAL**: When the write comes for new data points, they are serialized and compressed in a .wal file. The .wal is fsync'd and the data is added to the in-memory index before returning a success. The .wal files, each segments of 10MB size, start from _000001.wal and increase monotonically as more files are added. Each file is referred to as a WAL segment, and each such segment stores multiple compressed blocks of writes and deletes. When it reaches a certain number of points, then they are all flushed to disk storage as batches of 5000-10000 points, because of which it can achieve high-throughput performance. These data points are stored in the disk as TSM files which have compressed series data in a columnar format.

InfluxDB Data Elements and Schema

InfluxDB is a purpose-built time-series database that can handle large volumes of time-series data and is optimized to perform real-time analysis on that data. It is similar to SQL but has been built from the ground up specifically to handle the time-series workloads.

InfluxDB has constructs which are similar to SQL, and a comparison between the two will show that their data elements resemble this. Let's look at a few of the important concepts in InfluxDB in detail:

SQL Database	InfluxDB
Table	Measurement
Rows	Points
Indexed Columns	Tags
Unindexed Column	Fields
Stored Procedures	Continuous queries

In order to understand InfluxDB better, we have to take a deeper look into the InfluxDB schema. Data Explorer has an option of looking at the raw data which forms the InfluxDB table, as shown in Figure 5-47:

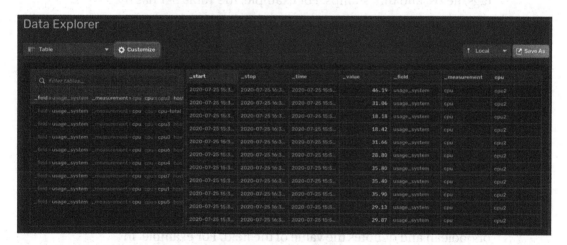

Figure 5-47. *InfluxDB data elements*

Rearranging the preceding table for clarity and adding some more values gives us Table 5-1:

Table 5-1. *InfluxDB Table*

_time	_measurement	Cpu	_field	_value
2020-07-25 T15:50:00Z	Cpu	cpu2	usage_system	46.19
2020-07-25 T15:51:00Z	Cpu	cpu2	usage_system	31.06
2020-07-25 T15:52:00Z	Cpu	cpu2	usage_system	18.18
2020-07-25 T15:53:00Z	Cpu	cpu2	usage_user	1.1
2020-07-25 T15:54:00Z	Cpu	cpu2	usage_user	1.89
2020-07-25 T15:55:00Z	Cpu	cpu2	usage_user	0.5

Measurement (_measurement): The measurement column in an InfluxDB table describes what the table is all about. Measurement is generally a string and acts as a container for other elements like tags, fields, and timestamps. For example, the Table 5-1 has the measurement **cpu**. This suggests that the table is related to the measurement of cpu metrics.

Timestamp (_time): Data is always stored in InfluxDB with a corresponding _time value. This is the timestamp of that data. Since it is a time-series database, date and time are usually stored in the RFC3339 UTC[9] format.

Field (_field): Field is generally a string that denotes the name of the field. In the preceding example, _field is usage_system.

Field value (_value): The field value can be string, integer, float, or boolean and denotes the value of the field. For example, in the first row, _field usage_system has a _value of 46.19 at that particular time.

Field set: The key/value pair of a field and its corresponding field value is termed as a field set.

Tag key: In the preceding example, the field **cpu** is the tag key.

---

[9]RFC3339 is the human-readable format for date and time (2020-01-01T00:00:00.00Z), used as timestamps in time series databases. For more details, please refer to `https://www.ietf.org/rfc/rfc3339.txt`.

Tag value: In the preceding example, the tag key **cpu** has multiple values like **cpu2**, **cpu3**, **cpu-total,** and so on.

Tag set: A tag set is the key/value pair of the tag key and the tag value. For example, cpu:cpu2 is a tag set.

Note   The difference between fields and tags is that fields are mandated in InfluxDB while tags are optional. So, your schema must have fields but you may or may not have tags. Then why do we need tags? Simply because fields aren't indexed whereas tags are. The queries which filter on the basis of field values will have to scan through all the values to return the result matching the query conditions because fields aren't indexed. However, queries on the basis of tags are much faster, as tags are indexed. Therefore, it is a common practice to store commonly queried data in tags.

Series key: A series key is made up of a measurement, a tag set, and a field key. So, taking reference from Table 5-1, we can create the following series:

_measurement	tag set	_field
Cpu	cpu=cpu2	usage_system
Cpu	cpu=cpu2	usage_user

Series: A series includes a timestamp and field values for a given series key. So, for a series key of

cpu, cpu=cpu2, usage_system

the series will be

2020-07-25 T15:50:00Z 46.19

2020-07-25 T15:51:00Z 31.06

2020-07-25 T15:52:00Z 18.18

Points: Points are made up of timestamps, series keys, and field values. So a single point from Table 5-1 would be the following:

Timestamp	measurement	tag set	field_value
2020-07-25 T15:50:00Z	Cpu	cpu cpu2	46.19

In comparison with a SQL database table, a row in SQL is a point in InfluxDB which represents a single data record with measurement, tag set, field set, and a unique timestamp. A point is uniquely identified by its series and timestamp. If a point is written with a timestamp that equals an existing point, then the old and new field sets will be merged, with any ties going to the new field set.

Tables

Now let us examine an InfluxDB table (see Figure 5-48):

- **Annotation rows:** Include #group, #datatype, #default and describe column properties.

- **Header row:** Includes _time, _measurement, _field, _value, tag, and so on. It defines column labels that describe the data in each column.

- **Data rows:** Contain data for one point.

- **Other columns:** Optional columns for annotation, result, and table.

- **Group keys:** Group records that share common values in specified columns.

Figure 5-48. *InfluxDB tabular data schema*

InfluxDB tabular schema is useful to analyze the metrics sent into InfluxDB as raw data and return the results of queries in annotated CSV format.

Line Protocol

InfluxDB uses a text-based format which includes measurement, tag set, field set, and timestamp to write data points. The syntax for line protocol is whitespace-sensitive, and individual lines which represent a single point in InfluxDB are separated by the newline character, \n. The syntax for line protocol is shown in the following:

```
<measurement>[,<tag_key>=<tag_value>[,<tag_key>=<tag_value>]]
<field_key>=<field_value>[,<field_key>=<field_value>] [<timestamp>]
```

For example, a single point as line protocol will look as follows:

```
myMeasurement,tag1=value1,tag2=value2 fieldKey="fieldValue" 1556813561098000000
```

So, a line protocol as depicted in the preceding consists of measurement, tag set, field set, and timestamp.

InfluxDB interprets the data point by way of whitespaces. The first whitespace helps InfluxDB to delimit measurement and tag set from the field set, whereas the second whitespace delimits the field set from the timestamp. Multiple tag sets can be used, but they need to be comma delimited.

Influx Query Language

Flux is the query language for InfluxDB designed for querying and analyzing the data.

To explain it better, let's start with an example. In the Script Editor in Figure 5-49, we are querying data stored from the last hour, filtered by the measurement cpu and the cpu=cpu-total tag, windowing the data in 1-minute intervals, and calculating the mean average of each interval.

```
Query 1 (0.07s)    +

1    from(bucket: "monitoringcloudnativeapps")
2      |> range(start:-1h)
3      |> filter(fn: (r) => r["_measurement"] == "cpu")
4      |> filter(fn: (r) => r["cpu"] == "cpu-total")
5      |> aggregateWindow(every: 1m, fn: mean)
6      |> yield(name: "mean")
```

Figure 5-49. *Script Editor*

As seen in this example query, Flux needs the following:

from: The from() function defines the data source from which data is to be collected. It requires the name of the bucket as an input parameter.

range: The range() function defines a specific time range from which to query the data collected from the data source. It requires two parameters: start and stop. However, the stop parameter can be omitted. Time ranges can be either relative or absolute. The relative time range uses negative duration, as it measures time in the past relative to the time now or the stop time, if that was added to the query. In the case of the absolute time range, you can enter timestamps.

filter: The filter() function filters data in columns based on the logic passed onto the parameter fn, where 'r' refers to the data in the rows.

yield: The yield () function outputs the data filtered as a result of the query. In case there are multiple queries being run in the same query, adding the yield () function becomes necessary.

pipe-forward operator: The pipe-forward operator '|>' is used to chain the functions together in a query in order to build sophisticated multifunction queries.

In the sample query used in Figure 5-49, the from () function is used to load the data from the monitoringcloudnativeapps bucket for the defined time range of the last 1 hour. The collected data is then filtered for row values of 'cpu' and 'cpu-total'. The filtered data is then aggregated for every 1-minute interval. The result is then yielded as the mean of the filtered values.

InfluxDB provides another way of writing query by using the **Query Builder,** as shown in Figure 5-50:

Figure 5-50. *Query Builder*

Query Builder is the UI equivalent of the Script Editor, and all the functions we saw earlier can be easily applied using the Query Builder as well.

Alerting

InfluxDB lets you create alerting rules which when breached can be configured to send notifications on your favorite notification endpoints. Let's go through the steps for how to configure alerts in InfluxDB.

1. Configure checks to monitor data and assign a status

2. Integrate a notification endpoint to send notifications

3. Create notification rules to check status and send notifications to notification endpoints

Configuring a Check

The first step is to configure checks, which can be easily created using the UI, as shown in Figure 5-51:

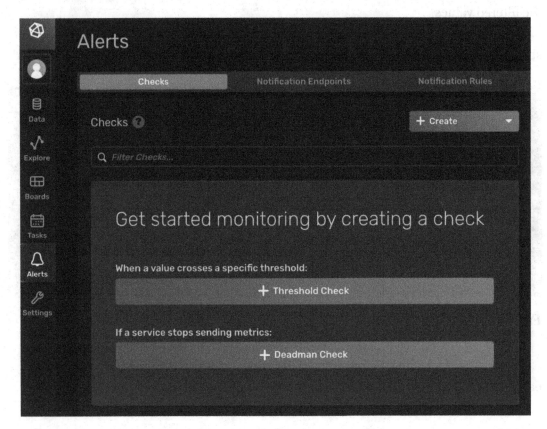

Figure 5-51. *Creating checks*

A check is a periodic query that InfluxDB performs against the time-series data to generate a status based on specific conditions and apply it to each point.

Checks are of two types:

- A threshold check applies a status based on the comparison with the threshold value. For example, a given field value is above, below, inside, or outside of defined thresholds.

- A deadman check assigns a status when there is no response from a series or group within a given amount of time.

A check consists of a defining a query and then configuring the check (see Figures 5-52 and 5-53). The query definition includes selecting the dataset which needs to be queried. The dataset would include measurement, field, and tags (optional). Using an aggregating function is mandatory for a valid check definition. Tags when included will help to narrow down the points to be queried.

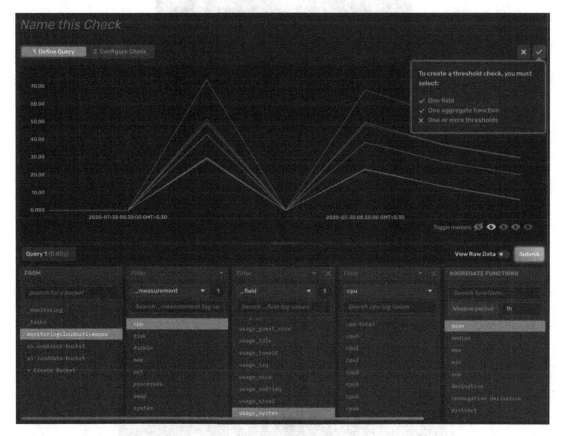

Figure 5-52. *Define query*

The second part includes configuring the checks in which we will define properties such as checking interval and the status message. In Figure 5-53, the check is scheduled to run every 5 minutes. You can also define a particular tag to be checked; in this case, the tag is cpu2.

Configure a Check
PROPERTIES
Schedule Every
Offset
5m
1m
Tags
cpu
=
cpu2
+ Tag

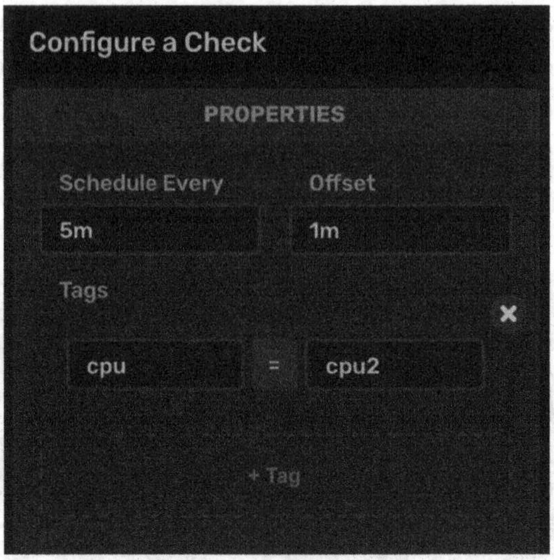

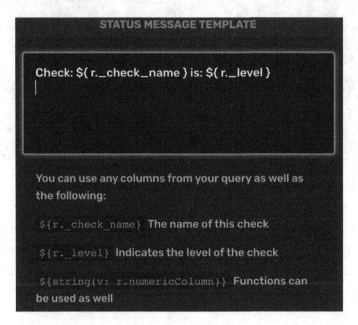

***Figure 5-53.** Defining properties for configuring a check*

You can also define the status message to be displayed in the status message template, as shown in Figure 5-54, which can include the check name and the level of the check in the given format.

STATUS MESSAGE TEMPLATE
Check: ${ r._check_name } is: ${ r._level }
You can use any columns from your query as well as the following:
${r._check_name} The name of this check
${r._level} Indicates the level of the check
${string(v: r.numericColumn)} Functions can be used as well

***Figure 5-54.** Status message template to be displayed in the case of an incident*

It then applies a status to each data point—CRIT, WARN, INFO, OK—if the specified condition evaluates to be true. These datapoints are called thresholds.

Setting Thresholds

Thresholds are classified into four levels, starting from OK all the way up to CRIT in increasing order of seriousness. See Figures 5-55, 5-56, and 5-57.

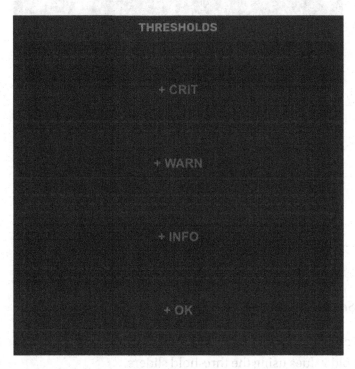

Figure 5-55. *Classification of thresholds*

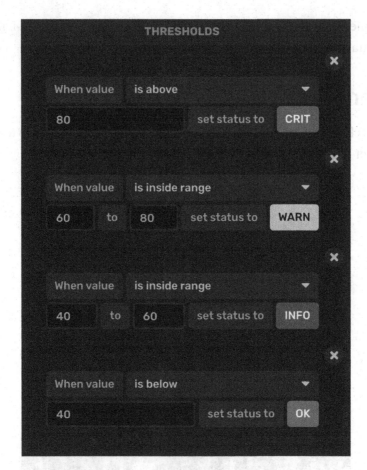

Figure 5-56. *Setting thresholds*

Thresholds can be set in absolute values or in ranges, or we can also use the sliders to define threshold values using the threshold sliders.

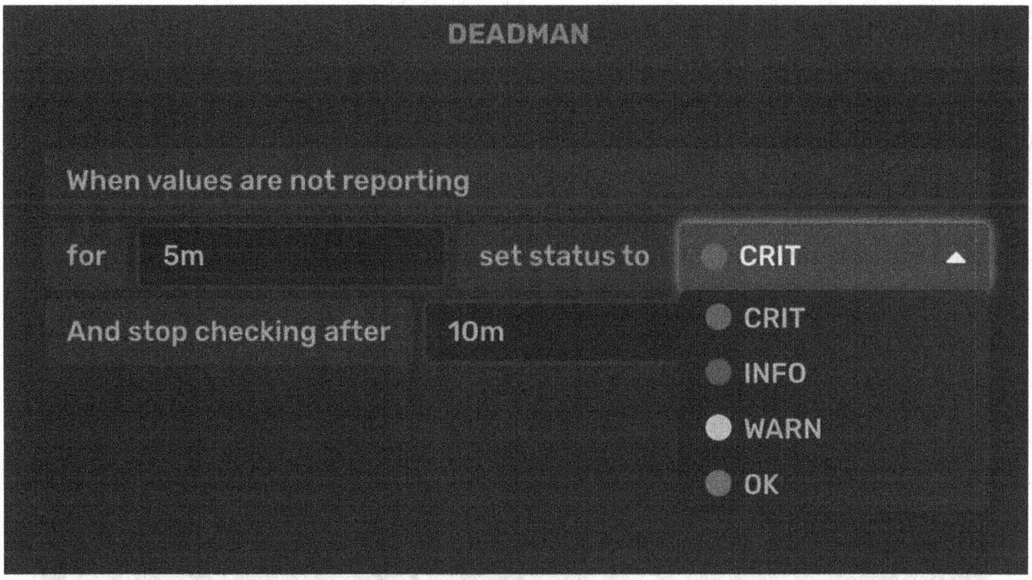

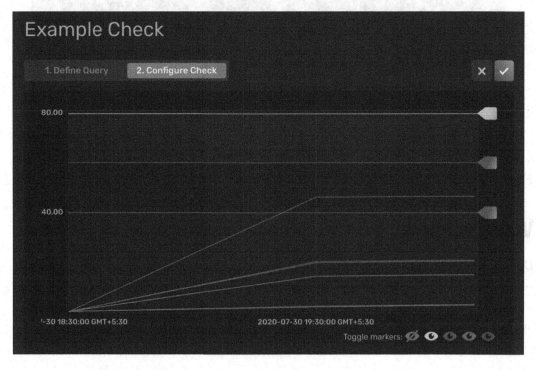

Figure 5-57. *Setting a deadman check*

Once you run the check, it should look like Figure 5-58. The threshold sliders can be set as desired from here as well; then click the green button to save.

Figure 5-58. *Threshold sliders*

Connecting to a Notification Endpoint

InfluxDB gives you an option to connect to a Notification Endpoint (see Figure 5-59) by configuring the following:

- HTTP server over a post method

- Slack via incoming Webhook

- Pagerduty using client URL and routing key

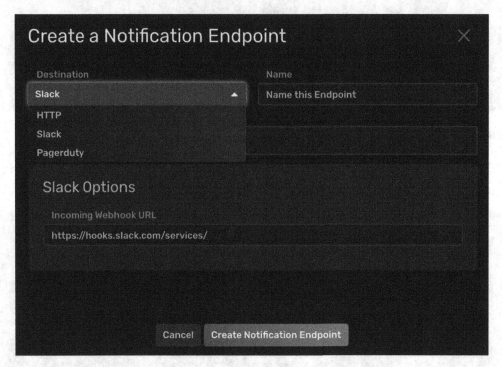

Figure 5-59. *Creating a Notification Endpoint*

Visualization

Dashboards are important assets in your day-to-day operations and provide you with a bird's-eye view of the state of your environment. You can visualize the metrics collected in InfluxDB through the UI using the dashboards. You can create custom dashboards either by importing JSON or from a pre-created template. See Figure 5-60.

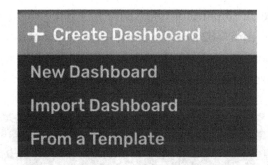

Figure 5-60. *Options to create a dashboard*

Let's explore the option of creating a dashboard from a template. We have the option of creating dashboards from the existing templates for Kubernetes, system data, and many others. In Figure 5-61, we have opted for dashboarding the metrics collected from InfluxDB itself. These metrics were collected using Scraper, which was discussed in detail in the "Data Collection" section.

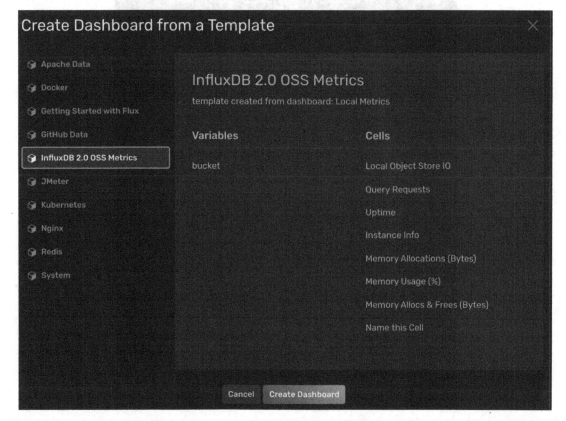

Figure 5-61. *Creating InfluxDB metrics dashboard from template*

Once you create the dashboard for InfluxDB 2.0 OSS metrics, you can see that the dashboard running in Figure 5-62 shows a running instance of the dashboard. So, the data collected by Scraper from InfluxDB itself is sent to the bucket, ui-explorer-bucket, and the dashboard reflects that data in a more meaningful form.

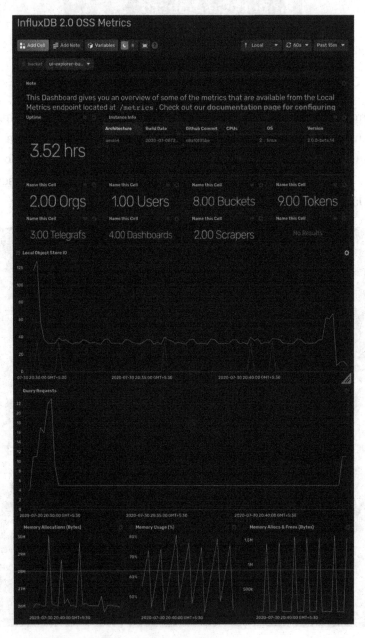

Figure 5-62. *InfluxDB 2.0 OSS metrics dashboard*

You can also use the template for system details to create a dashboard. This includes important system metrics like system uptime, CPU and memory usage, system load, and other critical details. Telegraf collects the relevant system metrics and stores them in the monitoringcloudnativeapps bucket and the dashboard can then help with the useful visualization of system stats.

A snapshot of the dashboard is shown in Figure 5-63:

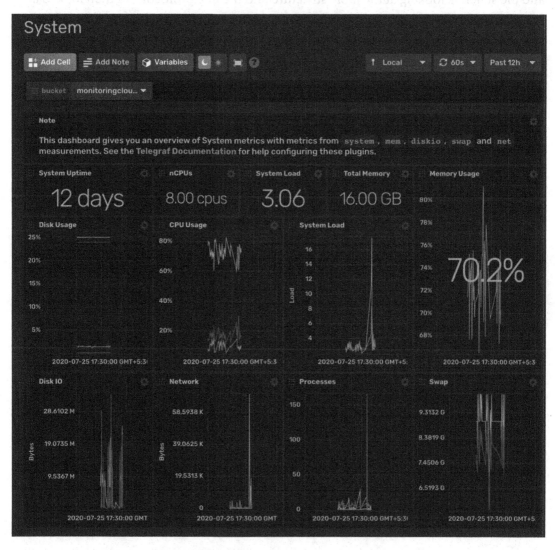

Figure 5-63. *Dashboard for Telegraf system plug-in*

Summary

This chapter has introduced us to the erstwhile TICK Stack, which is now renamed as InfluxDB. We learned about the architecture of InfluxDB and the key concepts that are essential to understanding InfluxDB. We also looked at the InfluxDB components for data collection: Scraper and Telegraf. We then took a deep dive into the data elements and the schema, looking at the table structure and the line protocol. We then looked at the influx query language, Flux, and the query syntax which can be used in the Script Editor or else to easily write queries using the Query Builder. We also looked at alerting and how to configure checks to notify you when thresholds are breached. In the end, we looked at the visualization options that are available to be used in InfluxDB.

We now have completed our learning of the second open source modern monitoring system, and in the next chapter we will talk about the multi-input visualization platform, Grafana.

CHAPTER 6

Grafana

Grafana is a popular open source time-series data query, visualization, and alerting tool which was developed by Torkel Ödegaard in 2014. It has a data source model which is highly pluggable and supports multiple time-series–based data sources like Prometheus, InfluxDB, and OpenTSDB as well as SQL databases like MySQL and Postgres. Independent of where the data is stored, it allows you to query the data using query editor, visualize it using dashboards, and alert on it using the alerting function.

Grafana was developed as an alternative to Kibana (part of ELK stack) as a time-series–based dashboarding tool focused on graphs. It was primarily designed to look good on TV in an operations control room with the thought that an operator would spend more time looking at it rather than tweaking it. When it started, it used to support InfluxDB and Graphite as the only two data sources. Now, Grafana is probably the only tool which supports combining data from many different sources into a single dashboard.

Features of Grafana:

- **Visualize:** The primary purpose of using Grafana is for visualization of metrics whether in the form of graphs, heatmaps, or histograms. Grafana provides numerous options to visualize your data with a choice for selecting themes and time zones.

- **Unify:** You can use over 30 data sources which Grafana supports to combine all the data your environment generates to create meaningful dashboards out of them. Besides having built-in support for Graphite, InfluxDB, Prometheus, Elasticsearch, and so forth, it provides an extensive set of data source plug-ins via its plug-in repository.

- **Extend:** Grafana has thriving community support which helps you extend beyond the out-of-box features to other third-party tools and platforms.

© Mainak Chakraborty and Ajit Pratap Kundan 2021
M. Chakraborty and A. P. Kundan, *Monitoring Cloud-Native Applications*,
https://doi.org/10.1007/978-1-4842-6888-9_6

- **Collaborate:** You can use the link to share Grafana dashboards with teams or publish them.

- **Alert:** By setting alerting thresholds, you can alert on critical situations with Grafana.

Grafana is not only available as an open source software but also as Grafana Enterprise and Grafana Cloud. Grafana Cloud is a fully managed Grafana instance running on public cloud and providing a highly available and highly scalable option to run your deployment along with long-term retention. If you would rather prefer to run and manage Grafana yourself with access to Enterprise-grade features, then Grafana Enterprise is the option for you. For the purposes of this book, we will restrict our discussion to the open source version of Grafana.

Installation

We will be installing Grafana on Kubernetes. Of course, there are other ways of running it starting from your local machine to docker and even ARM devices, but as we did with the other tools in Chapters 4 and 5, we will try and set it up in a Kubernetes cluster. The following installation steps assume that a Kubernetes cluster has already been set up. Readers are advised to use Minikube or Kind to set up a Kubernetes cluster by following instructions available at `https://kubernetes.io/docs/tasks/tools/`. We are running Minikube for setting up the Kubernetes cluster. You can use any managed or unmanaged Kubernetes deployment, but the installation process will be similar to the one described here.

Once Minikube is installed, start the Kubernetes cluster using the following command (see Figure 6-1):

```
$ minikube start
```

```
[mainakc ~ %minikube start
    minikube v1.12.3 on Darwin 10.15.7
    minikube 1.16.0 is available! Download it: https://github.com/kubernetes/minikube/releases/tag/v1.16.0
    To disable this notice, run: 'minikube config set WantUpdateNotification false'

    Using the docker driver based on existing profile
 !  Requested memory allocation (1998MB) is less than the recommended minimum 2000MB. Kubernetes may crash unexpectedly.
 !  Your system has 8192MB memory but Docker has only 2996MB. For a better performance increase to at least 3GB.

        Docker for Desktop  > Settings > Resources > Memory


    Starting control plane node minikube in cluster minikube
    Updating the running docker "minikube" container ...
    Preparing Kubernetes v1.18.3 on Docker 19.03.8 ...
    Verifying Kubernetes components...
    Enabled addons: dashboard, default-storageclass, storage-provisioner
    Done! kubectl is now configured to use "minikube"
```

Figure 6-1. *Starting the single-node Kubernetes cluster*

Once the Kubernetes cluster is up and running and kubectl has been installed successfully, the first thing to do is to list all the pods in the cluster using the following command (see Figure 6-2):

```
$ kubectl get pods -all-namespaces
```

```
[mainakc ~ %kubectl get pods --all-namespaces
NAMESPACE             NAME                                         READY   STATUS    RESTARTS   AGE
default               nginx-f89759699-5v46w                        1/1     Running   1          9d
kube-system           coredns-66bff467f8-n9jvm                     1/1     Running   1          9d
kube-system           etcd-minikube                                1/1     Running   1          9d
kube-system           kube-apiserver-minikube                      1/1     Running   3          9d
kube-system           kube-controller-manager-minikube             1/1     Running   5          9d
kube-system           kube-proxy-ghsd6                             1/1     Running   1          9d
kube-system           kube-scheduler-minikube                      1/1     Running   2          9d
kube-system           storage-provisioner                          1/1     Running   10         9d
kubernetes-dashboard  dashboard-metrics-scraper-dc6947fbf-g74dd    1/1     Running   1          9d
kubernetes-dashboard  kubernetes-dashboard-6dbb54fd95-xcthl        1/1     Running   2          9d
monitoring            prometheus-7f567bc485-4fjkr                   1/1     Running   0          3d4h
```

Figure 6-2. *List of pods*

Now, since the Kubernetes cluster is up and running and the monitoring namespace in which we will deploy Grafana is already created, we will deploy Grafana using a yaml file called grafana-deployment.yaml just like the one in Figure 6-3:

```
 1 apiVersion: apps/v1
 2 kind: Deployment
 3 metadata:
 4   labels:
 5     app: grafana
 6   name: grafana
 7   namespace: monitoring
 8 spec:
 9   replicas: 1
10   selector:
11     matchLabels:
12       app: grafana
13   template:
14     metadata:
15       labels:
16         app: grafana
17     spec:
18       containers:
19       - env: []
20         image: grafana/grafana:7.3.5
21         name: grafana
22         ports:
23         - containerPort: 3000
24           name: http
25         volumeMounts:
26         - mountPath: /var/lib/grafana
27           name: grafana-storage
28           readOnly: false
29       volumes:
30         - name: grafana-storage
```

Figure 6-3. *grafana-deployment.yaml file*

We have placed the file in the path where it can be accessed, and now we can create a deployment named "grafana" by using this file.

```
$ kubectl apply -f grafana-deployment.yaml
```

Once deployed, you can check that the Grafana deployment has been created, as shown in Figure 6-4.

```
[mainakc ~/Book/Grafana %kubectl apply -f grafana-deployment.yaml
deployment.apps/grafana created
```

Figure 6-4. *Grafana deployment created*

Let us look at the deployments across namespaces by using the following command (see Figure 6-5):

```
$ kubectl get deployments -all-namespaces
```

```
[mainakc ~/Book/Grafana %kubectl get deployments --all-namespaces
NAMESPACE             NAME                         READY  UP-TO-DATE  AVAILABLE  AGE
default               nginx                        1/1    1           1          9d
kube-system           coredns                      1/1    1           1          9d
kubernetes-dashboard  dashboard-metrics-scraper    1/1    1           1          9d
kubernetes-dashboard  kubernetes-dashboard         1/1    1           1          9d
monitoring            grafana                      1/1    1           1          2m15s
monitoring            prometheus                   1/1    1           1          3d5h
```

Figure 6-5. *List of deployments*

Also, let us have a look at the resources which are deployed in the monitoring namespace only. See Figure 6-6.

```
$ kubectl get all --namespaces=monitoring
```

```
[mainakc ~/Book/Grafana %kubectl get all --namespace=monitoring
NAME                              READY    STATUS     RESTARTS    AGE
pod/grafana-5bd86c74f6-hlw8t      1/1      Running    0           2m51s
pod/prometheus-7f567bc485-4fjkr   1/1      Running    0           3d5h

NAME                  TYPE        CLUSTER-IP      EXTERNAL-IP   PORT(S)          AGE
service/prometheus    NodePort    10.111.36.197   <none>        9090:30900/TCP   3d5h

NAME                          READY    UP-TO-DATE   AVAILABLE   AGE
deployment.apps/grafana       1/1      1            1           2m51s
deployment.apps/prometheus    1/1      1            1           3d5h

NAME                                       DESIRED   CURRENT   READY   AGE
replicaset.apps/grafana-5bd86c74f6         1         1         1       2m51s
replicaset.apps/prometheus-7f567bc485      1         1         1       3d5h
```

Figure 6-6. *List of resources in the monitoring namespace*

Since we don't have access to the resources that we created in the deployment, we will create a NodePort service that will provide us with the access to Grafana. See Figure 6-7.

```
 1 apiVersion: v1
 2 kind: Service
 3 metadata:
 4   name: grafana
 5   namespace: monitoring
 6 spec:
 7   selector:
 8     app: grafana
 9   type: NodePort
10   ports:
11   - name: grafana
12     protocol: TCP
13     port: 3000
14     nodePort: 30901
```

Figure 6-7. *grafana-nodeservice.yaml*

Let us deploy this file and create the NodePort service using the following command (see Figure 6-8):

```
$ kubectl apply -f grafana-nodeservice.yaml
```

```
[mainakc ~/Book/Grafana %kubectl apply -f grafana-nodeservice.yaml
 service/grafana created
```

Figure 6-8. *Creating a Nodeservice*

NodePort exposes the service on each node's IP at a static port (NodePort) default value, which is usually between 30000 and 32767. We can now look at Grafana on port 30901 of the single node. We can use the following command to open Grafana in a web browser.

```
$ minikube service -namespace=monitoring grafana
```

The output of the command is shown in Figure 6-9.

```
[mainakc ~/Book/Grafana %minikube service list --namespace=monitoring
|------------|------------|--------------------|-----|
| NAMESPACE  |    NAME    |    TARGET PORT     | URL |
|------------|------------|--------------------|-----|
| monitoring | grafana    | grafana/3000       |     |
| monitoring | prometheus | prometheus/9090    |     |
|------------|------------|--------------------|-----|
[mainakc ~/Book/Grafana %minikube service  --namespace=monitoring grafana
|------------|---------|--------------|--------------------------|
| NAMESPACE  |  NAME   | TARGET PORT  |           URL            |
|------------|---------|--------------|--------------------------|
| monitoring | grafana | grafana/3000 | http://172.17.0.2:30901  |
|------------|---------|--------------|--------------------------|
⋏  Starting tunnel for service grafana.
|------------|---------|--------------|--------------------------|
| NAMESPACE  |  NAME   | TARGET PORT  |           URL            |
|------------|---------|--------------|--------------------------|
| monitoring | grafana |              | http://127.0.0.1:53734   |
|------------|---------|--------------|--------------------------|
   Opening service monitoring/grafana in default browser...
!  Because you are using a Docker driver on darwin, the terminal needs to be open to run it.
```

Figure 6-9. *Getting the URL to access Grafana*

In the login screen shown in Figure 6-10, for the first-time login use the username and password as admin. You will be prompted to change the password to one of your own choice.

Figure 6-10. *Welcome screen for Grafana*

When you use the new password to log in, you should be able to see the welcome screen in Figure 6-11:

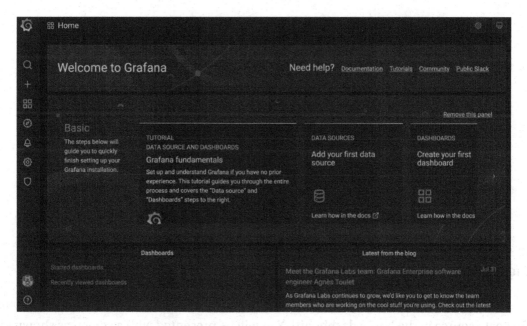

Figure 6-11. *Grafana home dashboard*

Now that you have a running instance, we will try and learn about the features and functionalities provided by the UI.

Adding a Data Source

Grafana doesn't come with its own agent and scrapers for data collection; however, it can easily integrate with several data sources, as most of the popular open source software comes as a core plug-in with grafan: time-series databases like Prometheus, Graphite, OpenTSDB, InfluxDB; logging and document databases like Elasticsearch and Loki; distributed tracing systems like Jaeger and Zipkin; SQL databases like MySQL and PostgreSQL; and public cloud monitoring tools like AWS CloudWatch, Google Cloud Monitoring, and Azure Monitor. See Figure 6-12.

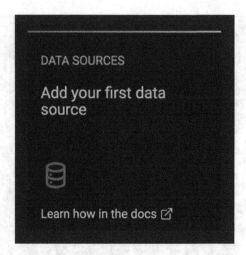

Figure 6-12. *Adding a data source*

You can start by adding data sources to Grafana by clicking the panel for adding your first data source in the home dashboard. You will be presented with a screen as shown in Figure 6-13:

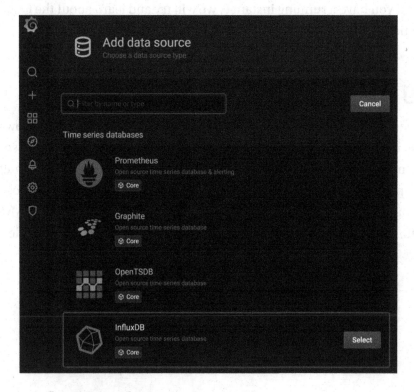

Figure 6-13. *InfluxDB as a data source*

From the list of data sources, let's try and integrate with InfluxDB. On the settings page, depending on the InfluxDB edition you are integrating with, you will have an option of choosing either InfluxQL or Flux as your query language of choice. We will go ahead with Flux, as we have InfluxDB 2.0 running. See Figure 6-14.

Figure 6-14. *Selecting a query language*

Then we will pass on the connection information so that InfluxDB can be reached from Grafana. We will also need to mention the organization, default bucket, connection token, and minimum time interval for Grafana to query InfluxDB. The default slider will mark InfluxDB as the default data source. See Figure 6-15.

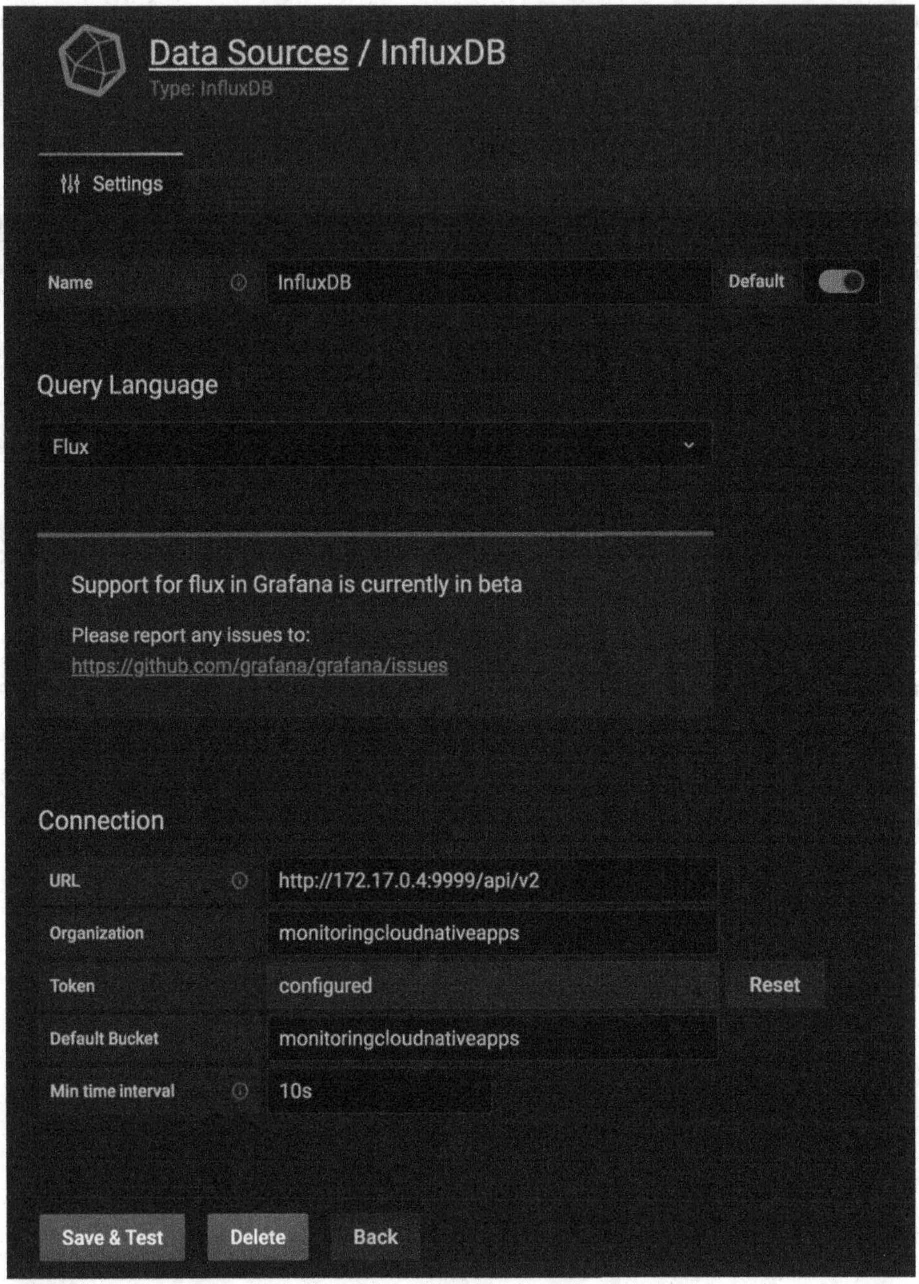

Figure 6-15. *Setting up InfluxDB as a data source*

Once you have saved and tested the data source, you will see the revised tile in the panel stating that the process of adding the first data source to Grafana has been successfully completed. See Figure 6-16.

Figure 6-16. *Data source successfully added*

Now, we will try to add another data source, Prometheus, by providing the necessary information. See Figure 6-17.

Figure 6-17. *Adding Prometheus as a data source to Grafana*

On saving and testing this connection, we should get a message that the connection has been successfully established. You should now be able to see the list of added data sources in the Configuration section. We have also added a prepopulated data base called TestData DB, which comes with Grafana. See Figure 6-18.

Figure 6-18. *List of data sources added in Grafana*

In the Prometheus data source page, you have the option of importing pre-created Prometheus dashboards as well. See Figure 6-19.

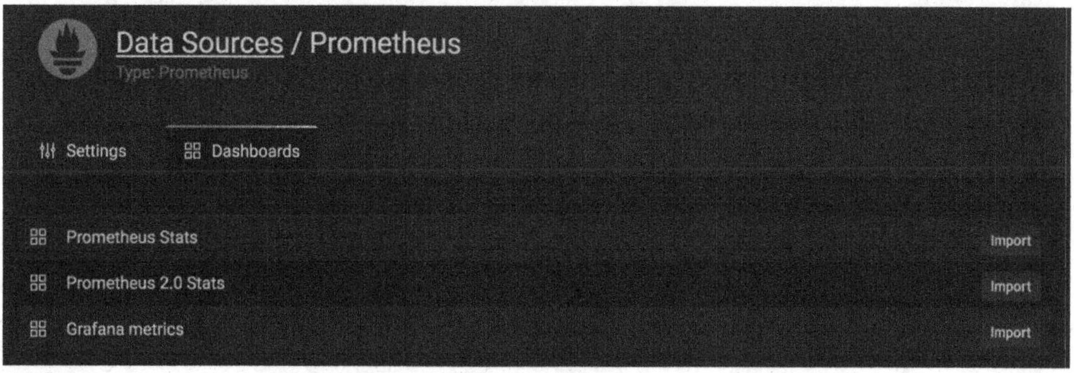

Figure 6-19. *Importing Prometheus dashboards*

These are detailed dashboards and can be used as a starting point for working with dashboards. You can also edit these dashboards and change the format if needed.

Creating a Dashboard

On the home dashboard for Grafana, another option is to create your first dashboard by clicking **Create your first dashboard** tile. See Figure 6-20.

Figure 6-20. *Creating a dashboard*

Panels

Before creating a dashboard, we have to learn about panels. A dashboard is made up of several panels, where each panel presents a particular type of information. Panels are therefore like building blocks which when put together will create a dashboard. Each panel has its own query editor, depending on the selected data source, which allows you to query for the information you want to visualize on the panel. See Figure 6-21.

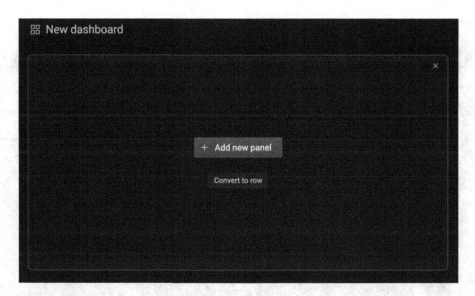

Figure 6-21. *Adding a new panel*

A panel is therefore a visual representation of results from one or more queries. In order to run queries, you must have a data source added. Once the query is executed, you can apply various formatting options to arrive at the perfect visualization as per your need. Panels can be arranged easily on the dashboard by dragging, dropping, and resizing them.

When you click **Add new panel** (shown in Figure 6-21), the new panel opens up the **panel editor**. Panel editor is also known as the Edit Panel screen or panel edit mode. You can also reach the panel editor by clicking an existing panel title drop-down and then selecting Edit, which opens the panel in edit mode. You can also click anywhere on an existing panel and press e to open it the panel editor.

Panel Editor

Once you add a panel, It will look like Figure 6-22. The various sections have been suitably marked for clearer understanding from a to f.

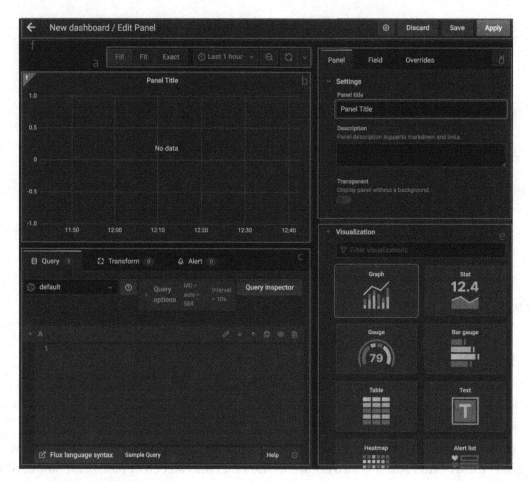

Figure 6-22. *Panel editor*

a) Visualization preview

- **Fill:** This option will fill the visualization preview with the space available in the preview pane. On resizing the sections, the visualization preview will adapt to fill the revised space available. See Figure 6-23.

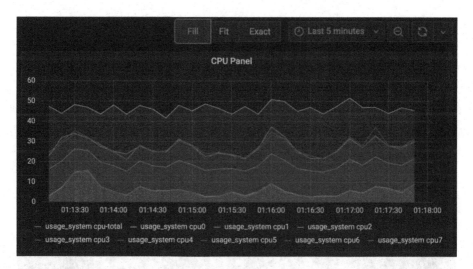

Figure 6-23. *Fill visualization preview*

- **Fit:** This option will fit the visualization preview in the available space preserving the aspect ratio of the panel. On resizing, it will try to restore the visualization preview to maintain the aspect ratio at all times. See Figure 6-24.

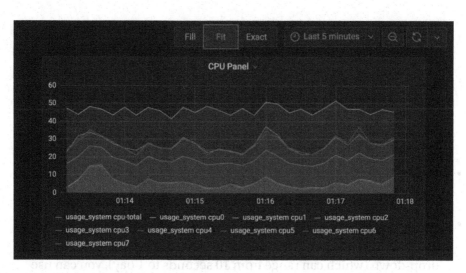

Figure 6-24. *Fit visualization preview*

- **Exact:** This option will resize the visualization preview to the exact size of the dashboard. In case, due to resizing of the panes, not enough space is available, it will scale down the visualization to preserve the aspect ratio. See Figure 6-25.

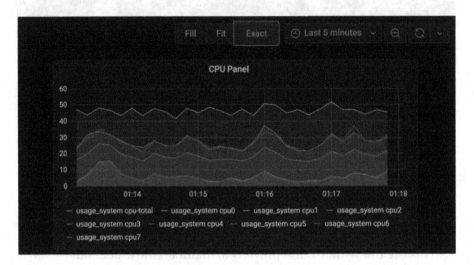

Figure 6-25.   *Exact visualization preview*

- **Time range controls:** This option helps you to select the suitable time range that you are interested in for the visualization preview.

- **Time range zoom out:** This small button in the shape of a lens, adjacent to the time range control, helps in zooming out the time window. With each successive click, you can have a wider time range under your inspection.

- **Refresh:** The Refresh button helps in manually refreshing the data for the selected time range.

- **Refresh dashboard interval:** If you want the data in the visualization preview to refresh automatically in an interval selected from the drop-down (which can range from 10 seconds to 1 day), you can use this option. It will fetch new data at an interval defined in the drop-down. You can also select the Off option in case you choose not to refresh the data automatically.

b) Panel title, axes, and legend

This section is the central piece of the panel and includes visualization as per the selected option. You can modify the panel title (highlighted in red box). The axes (in blue box) and legend (in green box) are derived from the query written in the query editor. In general, if we consider a single data point in a time series, the y axis denotes the field value and the x axis denotes the timestamp for that particular data point. When you combine several data points in a time-series database, you get a trendline as depicted in Figure 6-26:

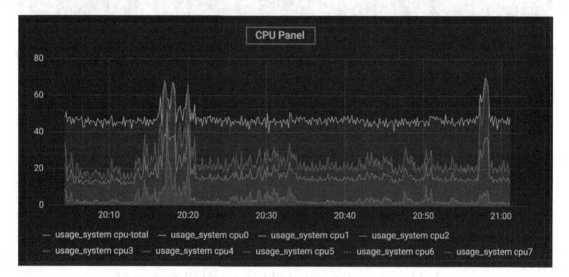

Figure 6-26. *Panel title, axes, and legend*

c) Data Section

One single query is needed for the panel to display a visualization. You can write one or more queries in the query editor. See Figure 6-27.

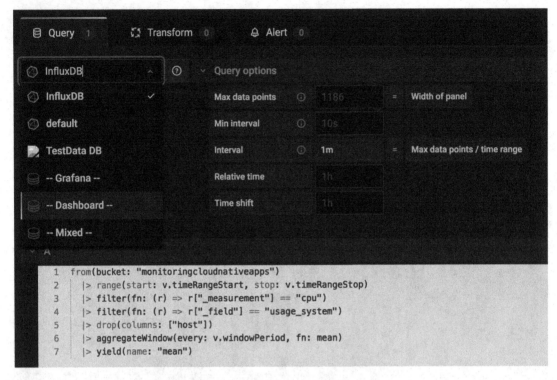

Figure 6-27. *Query editor*

In the Data Section - Query tab, you can select a data source from the list of integrated data sources and then write a query in the specific query language supported by that data source. The query language and its capabilities are different for each data source. In a single dashboard, we can have multiple panels all connected to different data sources but each panel can only be tied to one specific data source. You might want to apply data transformation in the Transform tab and set alert rules in the Alert tab.

d) Panel Settings, Field, and Overrides (see Figure 6-28)

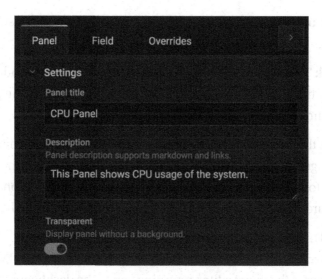

Figure 6-28. *Panel Settings*

Using the Panel Settings, you can add an appropriate panel title and a suitable description. The transparent slider will disable the dark background in the visualization panel.

e) Visualization

In this section, you can choose the way you want to display the data from the various options that Grafana provides for visualizing your query results. Refer to the "Visualization" section for more details.

f) Header

This section shows the dashboard name to which the panel belongs and some dashboard features. In order to return to the dashboard, just click the back arrow. See Figure 6-29.

Figure 6-29. *Header section*

- **Dashboard settings:** The gear icon is used to access the dashboard settings.

- **Discard:** This option will let you discard all the changes made to the panel, returning it to the last saved state. It will also close the panel editor and return you to the dashboard.

- **Save:** As the name implies, this option saves the dashboard with all the changes made in the panel editor till then. While saving, there is a tick box to save the current time range as the default for the complete dashboard. You can add a note describing the changes from the last save.

- **Apply:** This option will let you apply the changes made to the dashboard, but to persist those changes you have to save the dashboard. It then closes the panel editor, returning you to the dashboard.

Let's look at a panel for CPU usage of the system over the last 5 minutes (Figure 6-30).

Figure 6-30. *CPU panel*

The data source for the panel is InfluxDB (shown as default as we selected InfluxDB as the default data source during data source addition). In accordance with the data source, the query editor can use Flux as a query language. In the query editor, we have written a single query (A) to fetch data from the bucket monitoringcloudnativeapps. The time range is from a variable passed on for start and stop time. Then, we have included filters to filter data on the basis of _measurement = cpu and _field =usage_system. We are dropping the column host, as this information would be redundant since I am running this on a single host. Lastly, we are calculating a function (fn: mean) over the aggregating window, which is also a variable.

The result is visible in the form of line graphs depicting the CPU utilization of various CPUs like cpu0, cpu1, and so on. In order to inspect a particular line, you can hover over it and the tool tip displays field value and tag value at that instant.

Visualization

Grafana is renowned for its visualization prowess and the ease with which it can cater to any use case. In this section, we will try to explore all the different visualizations available in Grafana.

Stat

The Stat panel is one single dashboard which shows a particular stat value rather than the common line graph, although the option to add a graph is also there. This is important when one single value reveals the requisite information and the value from 5 minutes back might not be so relevant. For example, the total number of requests served will serve as a good stat value and not as a line graph. See Figure 6-31.

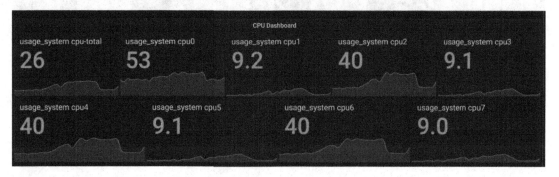

Figure 6-31. *Stat*

Gauge

Gauge is a common representation of a metric which provides a single number or data point corresponding to a current measurement at that time. Common metrics for utilization such as current CPU, memory, and disk usage are all represented as a gauge as the absolute value is of interest. See Figure 6-32.

Figure 6-32. *Gauge*

Bar Gauge

The bar gauge is a representation of every individual field as a single value. In Figure 6-33, the bar gauge captures the CPU usage percentages for various CPUs under consideration—CPU 1 to CPU 7 and overall CPU total.

Figure 6-33. *Bar gauge*

Display Settings

Display settings are available in the Panel section and offer various options to modify the visualization preview. We will explore the various settings available here. See Figure 6-34.

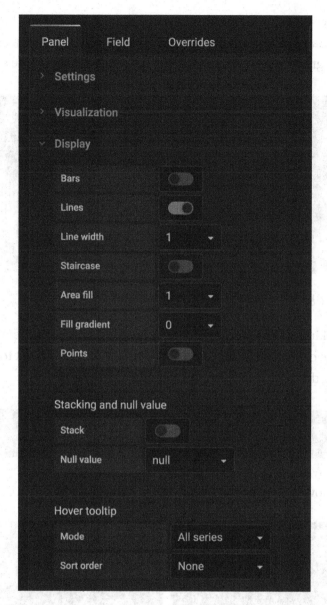

Figure 6-34. *Display settings*

The visualization section has the option of selecting the most appropriate visualization tool for the interpretation of the data. There are many options here, but sometimes the data which has to be displayed should be able to easily put across the idea of the graph and the dashboard. The most important suggestion doled out by monitoring experts is that it doesn't matter if your charts are beautiful; what matters is what they convey. So, selecting the right visualization is very critical.

Bars – A bar graph represents the same data as a line graph but uses rectangular bars to do so. When the slider for bar is active, the line graph will change to a bar graph, as shown in Figure 6-35:

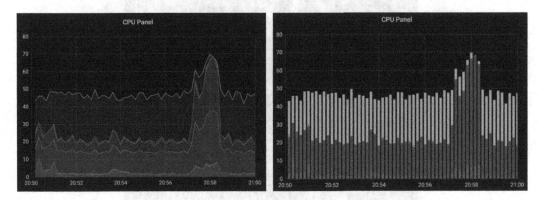

Figure 6-35. *Bar graph in comparison to a line graph*

Lines - Line graphs represent data in the form of a trendline. You have the option of changing the line width in case you want to vary the thickness of the line graph.

Figure 6-36 shows line graphs with varying line widths.

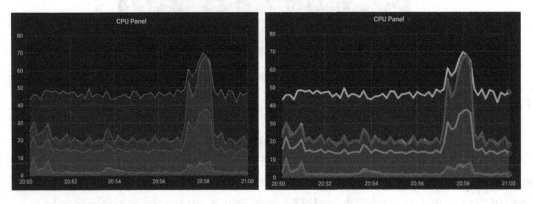

Figure 6-36. *Line graph*

Staircase - Staircase represents the same data as line graph but uses rectangular bars to do so. When the slider for Staircase is active, the line graph will change to a staircase, as shown in Figure 6-37:

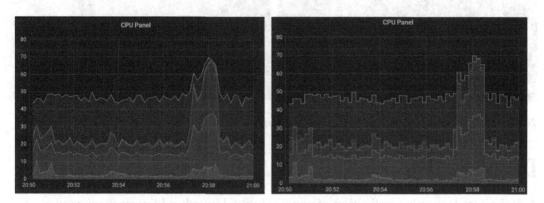

Figure 6-37. *Staircase in comparison to a line graph*

Area fill – This is used to convert the line graph into two-dimensional models. See Figure 6-38.

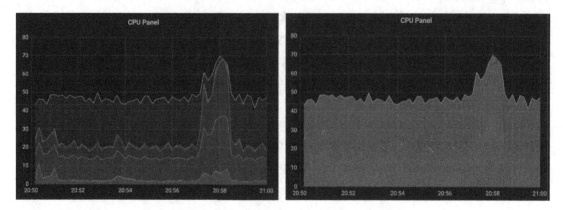

Figure 6-38. *Filling area in a line graph*

Fill gradient – This is similar to area fill, except in this case the area fill is in a gradient. You can choose a fill gradient from 0 to 10. See Figure 6-39.

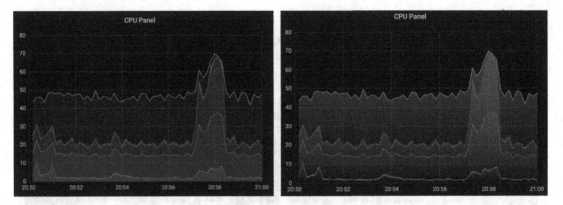

Figure 6-39. *Adding gradient to a line graph*

Dashboards

A dashboard is simply a collection of panels clubbed together to portray relevant information about a particular system or service in its entirety. They are created as per administrators' requirement to have updated information on the health and working of applications or services on a real-time basis. For example, a developer would be looking at the application performance and associated latency in the dashboard, whereas operations teams would be interested in looking at health parameters like the resource contention of the underlying system. It is very important to create a dashboard which can present data succinctly without grinding into too many details, so as to lose the context. You can always get into the logs for a detailed analysis after identifying the areas of concern through the dashboard.

Dashboards can be created from the Side menu bar using the Create (+) option and then clicking Dashboard. This will take you to a new blank dashboard; then follow the steps outlined earlier in the section on "Creating a Dashboard." See Figure 6-40.

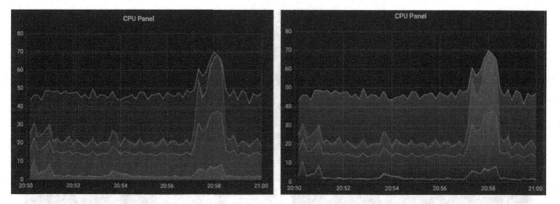

Figure 6-40. *Creating a dashboard*

The second option in the drop down menu is **Folder**. Folders provide a useful way to categorize your dashboards when you have multiple users and teams working on the same Grafana interface.

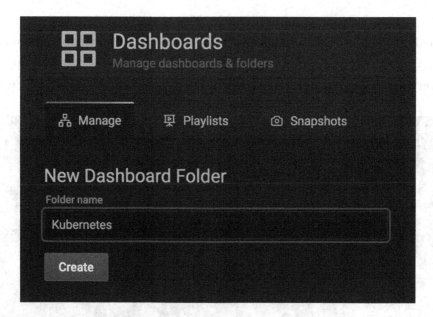

Figure 6-41. *Creating a folder*

Clicking Folder will open up a new window, as seen in Figure 6-41. You can provide a name for your folder based on the group of dashboards you want to create. In this case, we are creating a folder for all Kubernetes-related dashboards with the folder named Kubernetes. On clicking Create, we will be presented with another window, as seen in Figure 6-42:

217

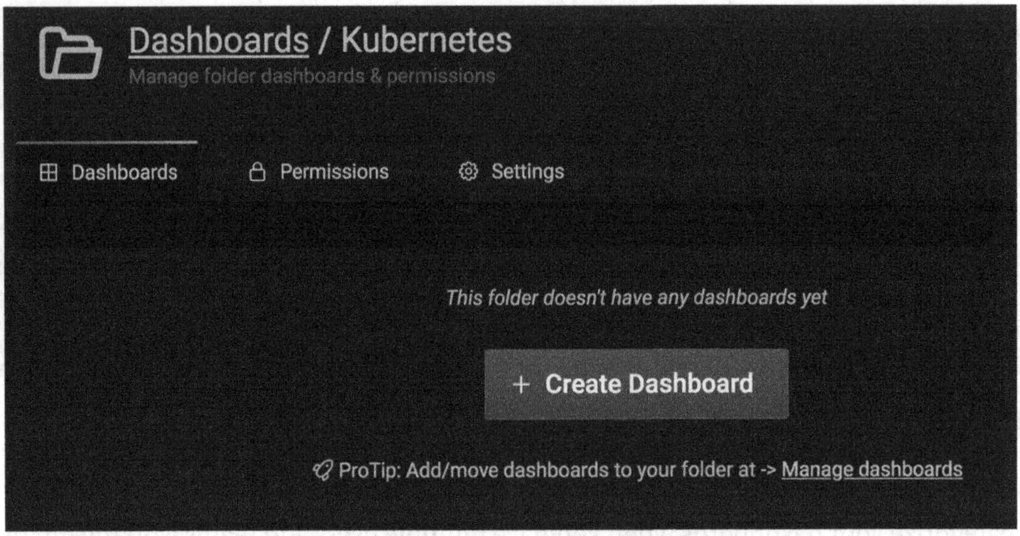

Figure 6-42. Kubernetes folder for dashboards created

You can create dashboards from within the folder itself by clicking **+ Create Dashboard**. You can also add permissions to the folder basis the entitlement for each user in a team. You can also add permission on the basis of role. For example, you might want to give everyone a view-only access to the folder and its dashboards. See Figure 6-43.

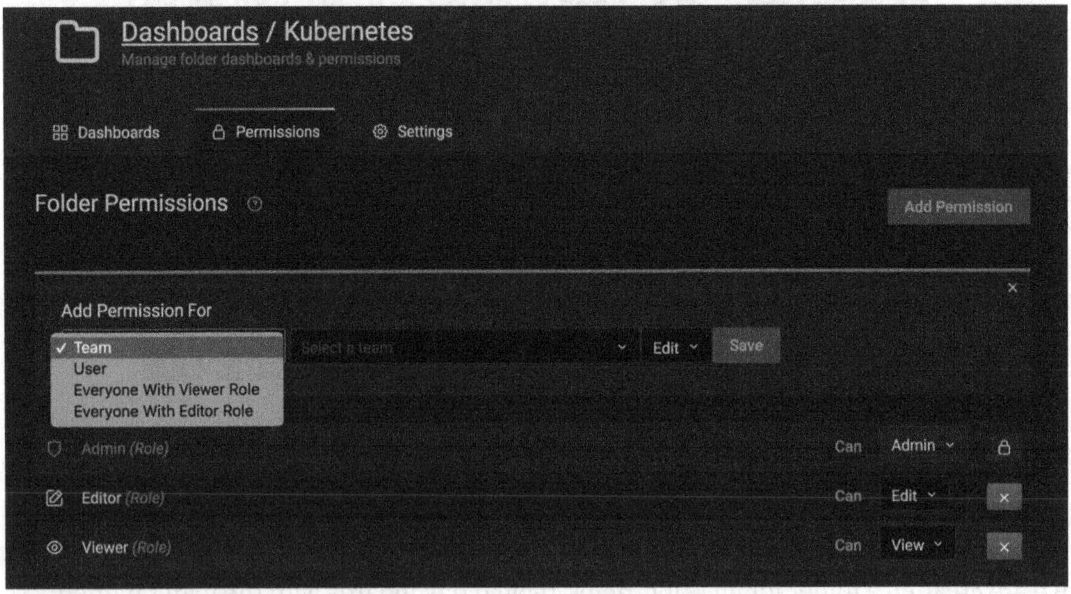

Figure 6-43. Folder-level permissions

The permissions you set at a folder level percolates to its dashboards. Only Grafana admins and super admins can create, edit, or delete folders.

The third option in the drop-down menu is **Import**, which you can use to upload a dashboard in JSON format, or use any of the various dashboards available at Grafana. com, or just paste JSON into the text box provided. See Figure 6-44.

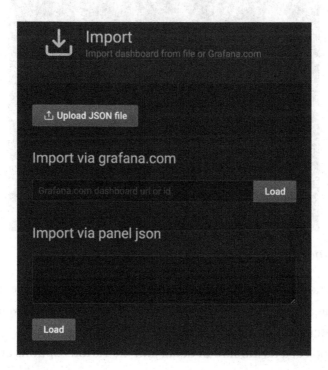

Figure 6-44. *Import dashboard*

When you select the option to upload a JSON file, after selecting the file, you are presented with the second step of the import process, in which you can modify the name of the dashboard, choose a folder to place your dashboard, and associate a unique identifier (UID) with the dashboard. See Figure 6-45.

Figure 6-45. *Importing JSON file*

Once importation is successful, you can find this dashboard in the Manage Dashboard section and inside the Kubernetes folder. We will look at Manage Dashboards option in detail later.

Now we will look at a dashboard in detail and the various options available to a user.

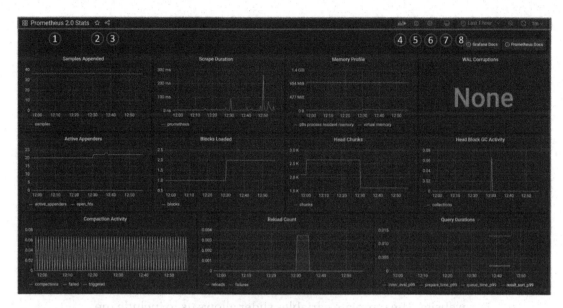

Figure 6-46. *Prometheus dashboard in Grafana*

This Prometheus dashboard comes bundled when you integrate Grafana with a Prometheus data source. The dashboard shows some very important information regarding the Prometheus instances and their functions, such as scrape durations and query durations.

Dashboard Header

In Figure 6-46, we have highlighted **Dashboard Header** and will go through the available options in detail by referring to the number highlighted in the figure.

1. Dashboard name - Shows the name of the dashboard you are currently viewing.

2. Mark as favorite - Favorite dashboards will appear on the Home tab.

3. Share dashboard - Share using direct link or snapshot, or export as JSON. See Figure 6-47.

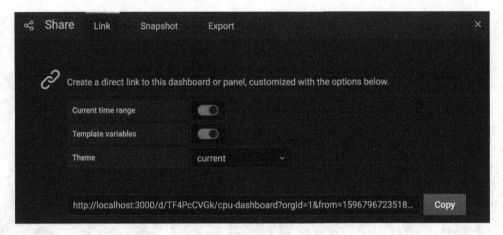

Figure 6-47. *Sharing dashboard through a direct link*

You can share this dashboard using the direct link or embed the link in a website. The template variables slider allows us to include the variables while sharing the dashboard with another user. You can also choose to modify the theme of the dashboard from dark to light.

You also have an option of taking a snapshot of the dashboard and then sharing it as an attachment. See Figures 6-48 and 6-49.

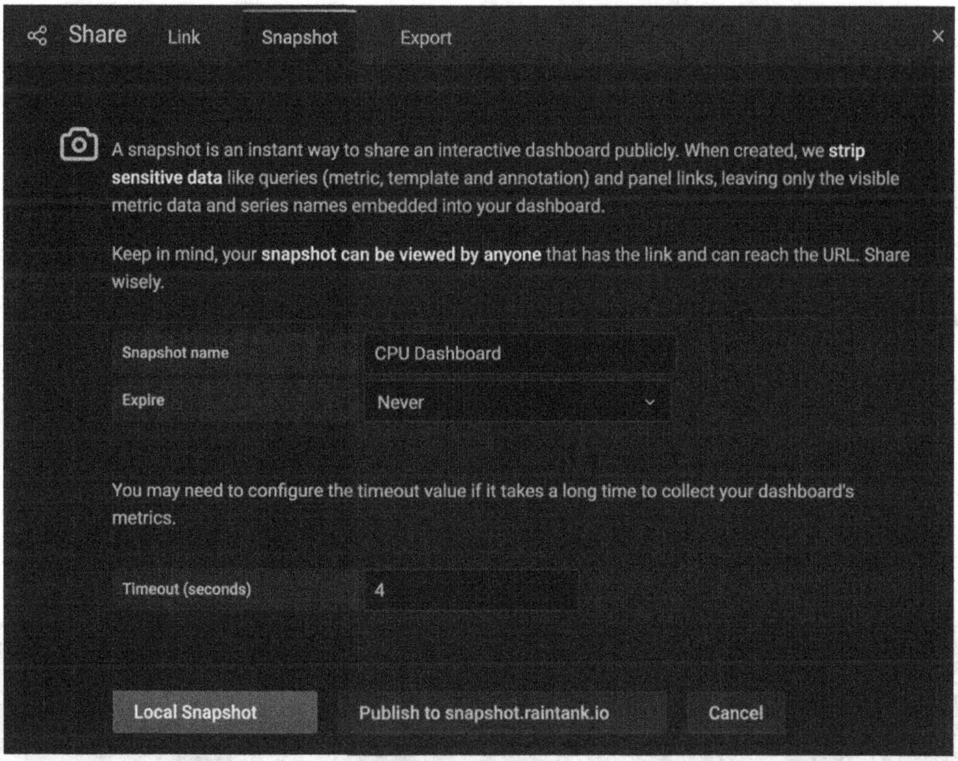

Figure 6-48. *Snapshot of a dashboard*

Figure 6-49. *Local snapshot link*

One more option is to export the dashboard as a JSON file using the
Export feature. You can view the JSON file by using the View JSON
option, which opens the dashboard in a JSON format and allows you
to copy the content on a clipboard. See Figure 6-50.

Figure 6-50. *Exporting dashboard as a JSON file*

Add a panel - You can add a panel to your dashboard by clicking the Add Panel button. It will add a blank panel to the dashboard with the default data source selected. You can rearrange your panels, edit the panel to connect it to a data source other than the default one, and run your queries on the data. See Figure 6-51.

Figure 6-51. *Adding a panel to a dashboard*

4. Saving a dashboard (Figure 6-52)

Figure 6-52. *Save dashboard option*

Once you click the Save dashboard option, a new window will pop up. You can enter the dashboard name and the folder where you want your dashboard to be placed. You can also copy the tags from the folder to the dashboard if that is what you need using the slider provided. When done, you can click Save. See Figure 6-53.

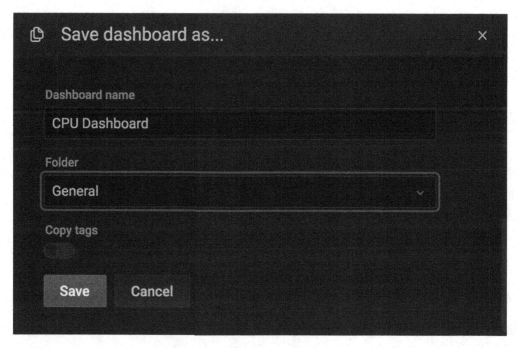

Figure 6-53. *Entering dashboard name and folder*

5. Cycle view mode - This option is used to change the display from normal mode to kiosk mode and kiosk TV mode. This is useful if you want to project the data in a Control Center environment.

6. Time picker drop-down -

    You have the option to change the time range of the dashboard. You can choose Absolute Time Range, where you can pick a start date and end date from a calendar, or Relative Time Range, where you can select from the available time durations. The option to change the time zone from UTC to local time is also available. See Figure 6-54.

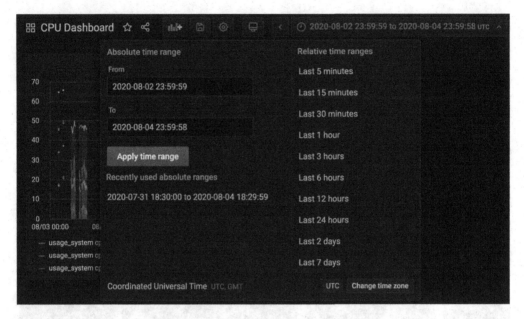

Figure 6-54. *Changing the time range of a dashboard*

Rows

A row is used to logically segregate your dashboard into specific areas so that a set of panels can be grouped together. If you save a dashboard with a row collapsed, then it saves in that state and does not load those graphs until you expand the row. Use the repeating rows functionality to dynamically create or remove entire rows, which can be filled with panels, based on the template variables selected. Once the row is created, it will look like Figures 6-55 and 6-56:

Figure 6-55. *Creating a row and assigning it a title*

Figure 6-56. *Row created*

Manage Dashboards

Grafana provides an option to manage dashboards, which is useful when you have several of them. See Figure 6-57.

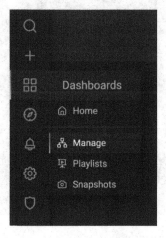

Figure 6-57. *Manage Dashboard option from side menu*

In the **Manage Dashboard** option, you can do several tasks like creating a new dashboard, creating a new folder, and importing a dashboard, all of which we have discussed earlier. You can also select a particular dashboard to move it to another folder or delete it. Notice that some dashboards have one or more tags associated which are nothing but key/value pairs that can help in organizing dashboards with the same tags together. You can also reach the dashboard folder page by clicking the cog icon, which appears when you hover over any folder in the dashboards list. See Figure 6-58.

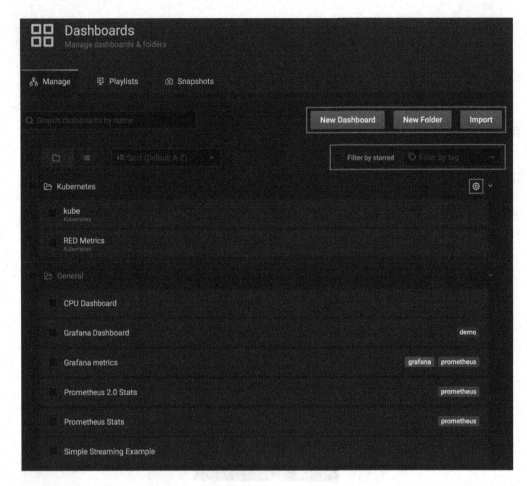

Figure 6-58. *Manage Dashboards*

Dashboard Folder

The dashboard folder page is where you can find in one place all the dashboards pertaining to that folder. It allows you to create a new dashboard or import dashboards. You can also select a particular dashboard either to move it to another folder or to delete it. On this page, you can also set permissions on a folder level in the Permissions tab, which are then cascaded to the dashboards, or you can rename a folder in the Settings tab. See Figure 6-59.

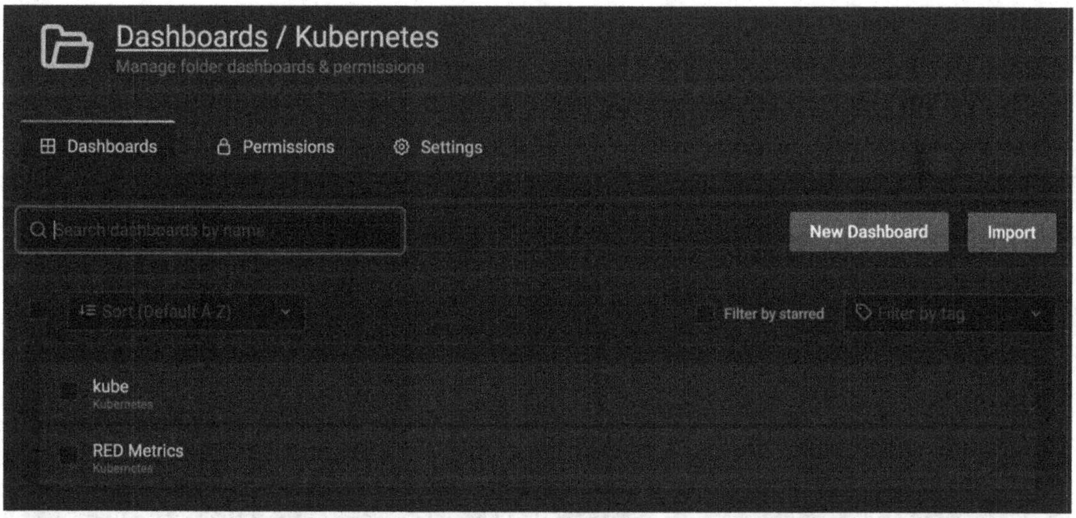

Figure 6-59. *Dashboard folder page*

Playlists

Playlist is a sequence of dashboards ordered to play sequentially at a particular time interval. This feature is commonly used to project the information on the dashboards to the big screen in an operation control room where your operators sit. Grafana handles the resolution and the scaling part, making the dashboards perfect for big screens. The playlist feature can be accessed from the dashboard submenu. See Figure 6-60.

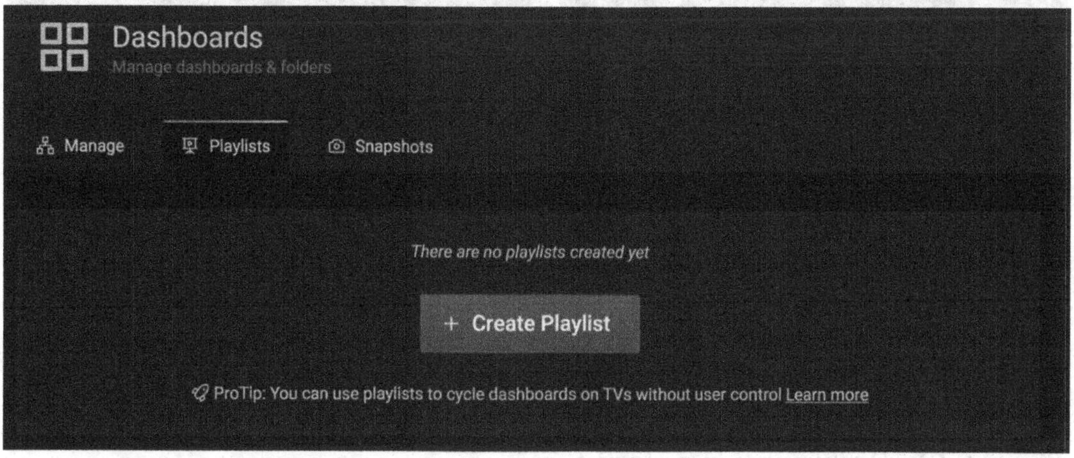

Figure 6-60. *Creating a playlist*

The interval is the time after which each of the dashboards will be refreshed with another dashboard from the playlist. Once started, a playlist can be controlled using the navigation bar at the top of the screen. A playlist can be run in five different modes, which determine the position of the menu and the navigation bar on the dashboard. The various modes are normal mode, kiosk mode, kiosk mode with auto-fit panels, TV mode, and TV mode with auto-fit panels. See Figures 6-61 and 6-62.

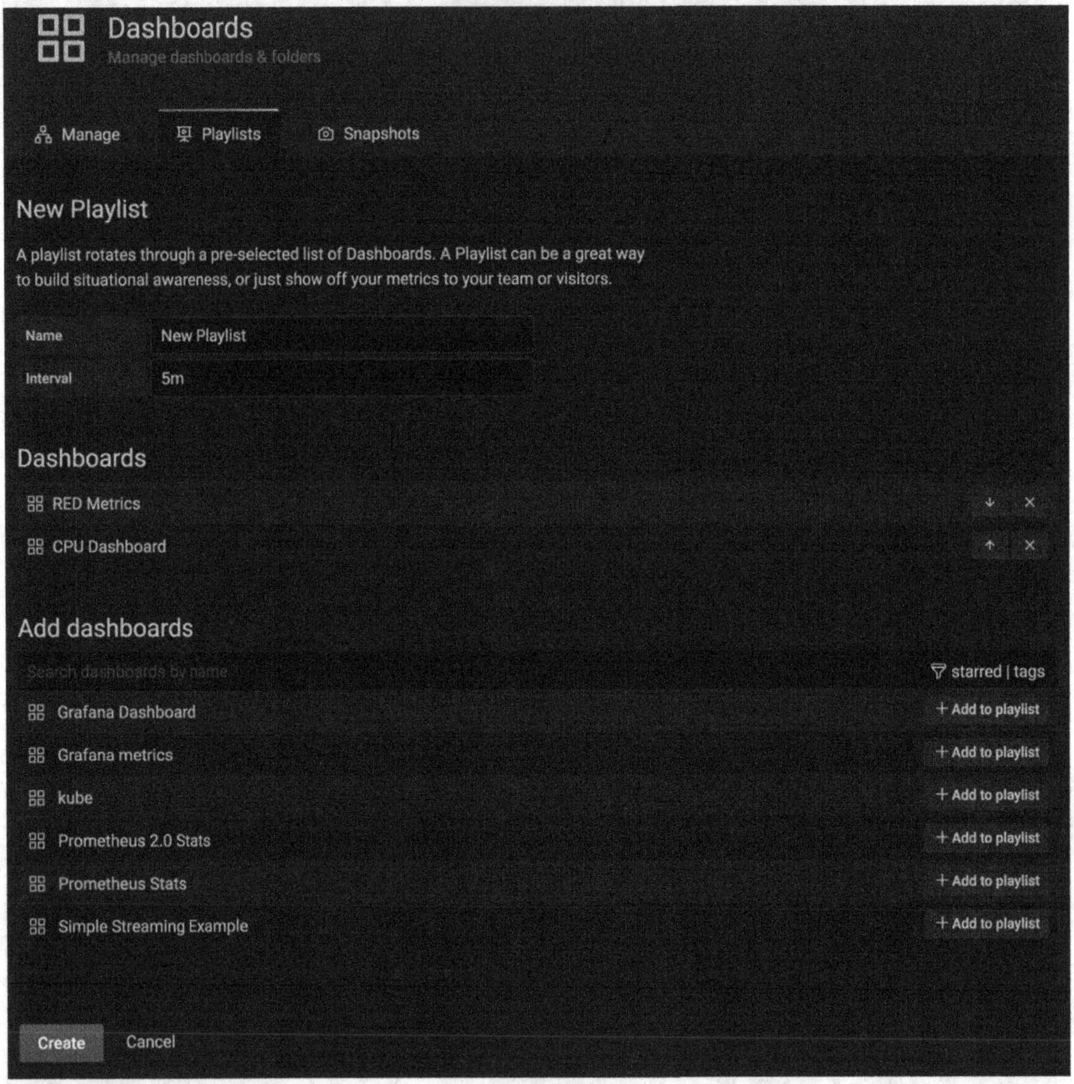

Figure 6-61. *Dashboards in a playlist*

Dashboards
Manage dashboards & folders

Manage   Playlists   Snapshots

Name   Snapshot url

CPU Dashboard   http://localhost:3000/dashboard/snapshot/40ntl4774zjNbPWKaZzmytgFEZOOsoP5   View   ×

Figure 6-62. *Snapshots*

Explore

Explore is a stripped-down version of the dashboard, where you can work with your
query around metrics, logs, and traces. Once you are satisfied with the query, you can
build a dashboard or graph out of it. This is beneficial when you want to work on a
complex query with proper focus and not think about how to present the results. See
Figure 6-63.

Figure 6-63. *Explore menu*

Explore allows you to run multiple queries and correlate the results. It can work with
metrics, logs, and traces and can help you get an end-to-end view into your monitoring
data. Loki, which is Grafana's logging data source, is tightly integrated with Explore and
allows correlation of data in one single console. See Figure 6-64.

231

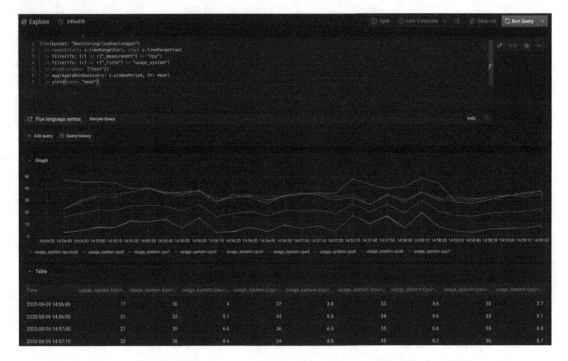

Figure 6-64. *Explore section*

Alerting

Alerts notify you when the state of your system changes based on some predefined conditions which Grafana regularly checks against. If one or more of these conditions are triggered, you can choose to get notified on the channels configured to receive notifications. Once you are notified of the problem, you can look into the problem and use Grafana to identify the cause and resolve the issue.

You can start creating alerting rules in the Alerting section, which is accessible from the side menu bar of Grafana (Figure 6-65).

Figure 6-65. *Alerting section*

In this section, you can view all the existing alerts with their corresponding states, but to create alerts, let's go back to the dashboard graph panel and the query editor. The third tab is used to create an alert by clicking the button provided (Figure 6-66).

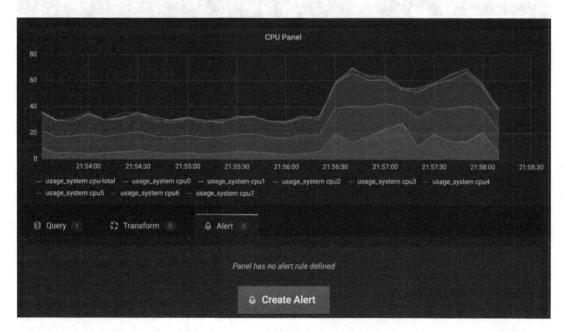

Figure 6-66. *Creating an alert*

You can now configure the alert by setting the condition to be evaluated. In Figure 6-67, we are evaluating for the condition the when average of the query is above a value of 65. The condition is set to be evaluated every minute for a total of 5 minutes.

Grafana will send no notifications when the query threshold of 65 is breached, but will only change the alert state from OK to pending. If the query result remains above 65 for a duration equal to 5 minutes, it will automatically change the alert state from pending to alerting and send alert notifications.

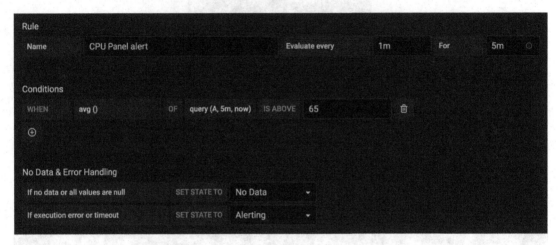

Figure 6-67. *Setting an alert rule*

Now once we have created the alert rule, next step would be to set up an alert rule notification. In this section you can add the notification channel (like email) to which a notification will be sent in case an alert rule changes to the alerting state. You can add a message describing the alert and possible steps to resolve the issue. You can also add tags to an alert in case you want to classify it in a particular category, which would be helpful later to analyze which type of alerts get generated more than others. See Figure 6-68.

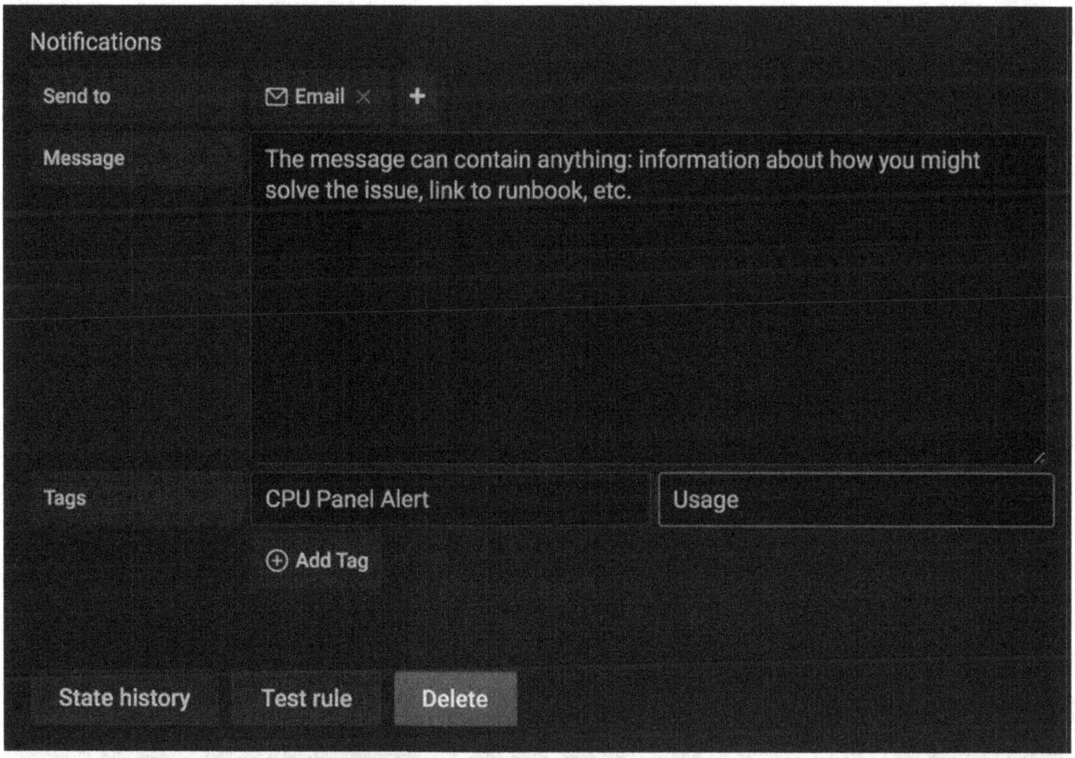

Figure 6-68. *Setting alert notifications*

Grafana has a scheduler and query execution engine where alert rules are evaluated. It supports only a limited number of data sources like Prometheus, InfluxDB, Elasticsearch, and so forth. In case you have deployed Grafana in a highly available setup, all the servers will execute the alerts, but alert notifications will be deduped, sending out a single notification only.

State History

The changes in the state of an alert are tracked in an internal table in Grafana's database. As seen in Figure 6-69, the last 50 state changes from **OK** to **ALERTING** are captured with date and time. You can also clear the state history by clicking the Clear History button. The state changes are marked in the graph panel as annotations.

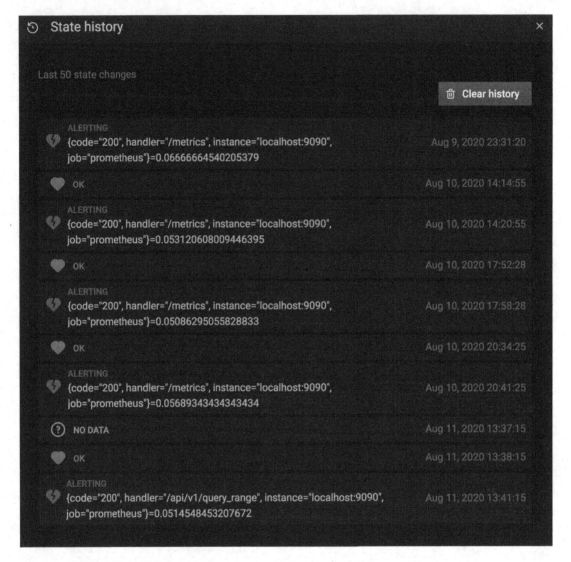

Figure 6-69. *State history*

Test Rule

It is important to check if the alert rule you have configured works as intended or not. You can test the alert rule you have configured by clicking Test Rule. In case the rule works as intended, you would be able to see these parameters: firing: true and conditionEvals: "true = true". Since the alert rule is active, the state should be shown as 'alerting.'

As shown in Figure 6-70, there are two more sections where you can find more details on the alert which is firing. One section shows the object which is satisfying the alert rule. In Figure 6-70, it's the handler="/metrics" which has a value greater than the configured alert threshold for 0.5. The second section is for logs, which shows that the value for the object handler="/metrics" is higher than the threshold limit of 0.5.

```
⚙ Testing rule                                                                    ✕

▼Object                                                    ⊕Expand All   ⎘Copy to Clipboard
  firing: true
  state: "alerting"
  conditionEvals: "true = true"
  timeMs: "6.346ms"
  ▼matches: Array[1]
    ▼0: Object
      metric: "{code="200", handler="/metrics", instance="localhost:9090", job="pr
      ometheus"}"
      value: 0.0666666879320257
  ▼logs: Array[16]
    ▼0: Object
      message: "Condition[0]: Query"
      ▶data: Object
    ▼1: Object
      message: "Condition[0]: Query Result"
      ▶data: Object
    ▼2: Object
      message: "Condition[0]: Eval: false, Metric: {code="200", handler="/api/v1/l
      abel/:name/values", instance="localhost:9090", job="prometheus"}, Value: 0.
      000"
      data: null
    ▼3: Object
      message: "Condition[0]: Eval: false, Metric: {code="200", handler="/api/v1/m
      etadata", instance="localhost:9090", job="prometheus"}, Value: 0.000"
      data: null
    ▼4: Object

    ▼9: Object
      message: "Condition[0]: Eval: true, Metric: {code="200", handler="/metrics",
      instance="localhost:9090", job="prometheus"}, Value: 0.067"
      data: null
```

Figure 6-70. *Testing the configured alert rule*

Once the alert is successfully configured, it will appear under the **Alert Rules** tab in the **Alerting** section as seen in Figure 6-71.

Figure 6-71. *Alert rule firing*

Adding a Notification Channel

A notification channel is the medium where you want to be notified instantly whenever your monitoring system generates an alert. In order to receive notifications in your favorite notification channel, integrate it first with Grafana from the Notification channels tab. See Figure 6-72.

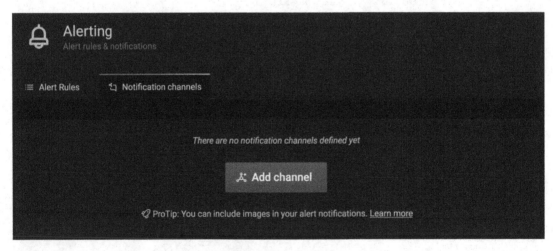

Figure 6-72. *Adding a notification channel*

Grafana supports many popular notification channels, including OpsGenie, PagerDuty, Slack, and email. In the **New Notification Channel** page, select the **Type** of notification channel and configure the settings. In Figure 6-73, we have selected an email notification type and added the addresses which are to be notified in case of an alert. You can also send a test mail to validate the configuration.

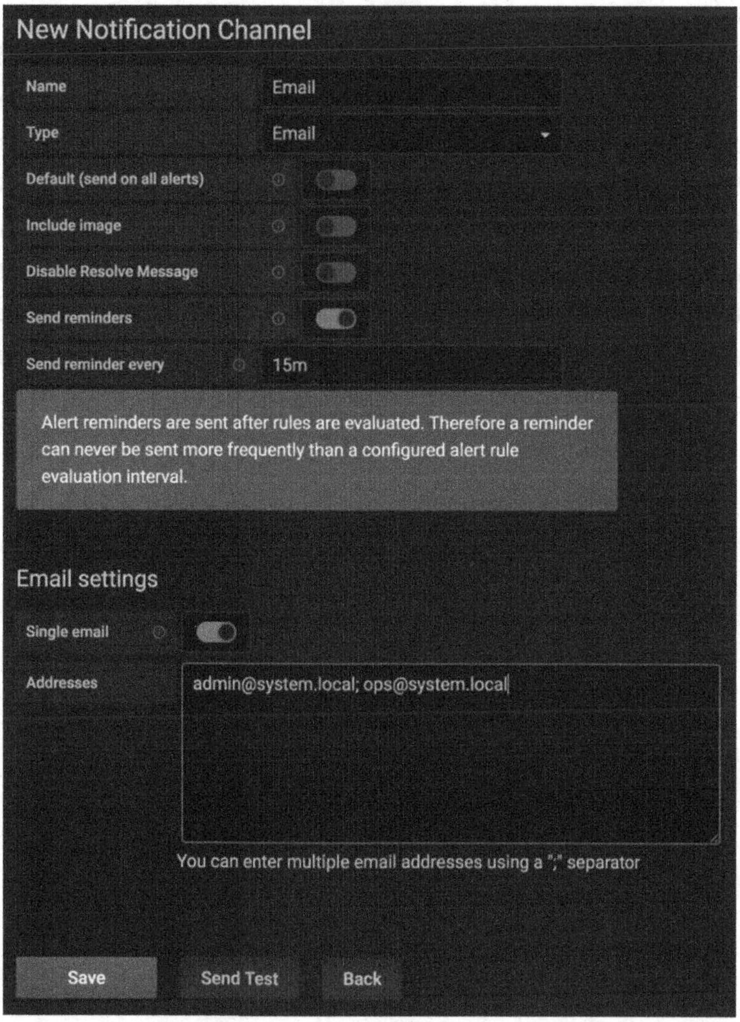

Figure 6-73. *Adding a new notification channel*

Summary

In this chapter, we learned about the visualization aspects of a modern monitoring system in detail. We looked at how Grafana can be that back end for visualization no matter what data collection mechanism you may have at the front. We tried our hands at creating dashboards using the various components available in Grafana. We discussed the visualization options that Grafana provides. In the end, we looked at the alerting engine available and how we can get notified about a problem using a notification channel of our choice. Grafana gives us a mechanism to understand our cloud native applications better and therefore improve them, if the opportunity presents itself.

Now, by the end of this book, the reader should have gained a solid grasp on popular open source tools like Prometheus, InfluxDB (TICK Stack), and Grafana. The reader should also have a good understanding of which tool to choose for which use case. Hopefully, with this new knowledge you will be able to lead agile operations for your organizations confidently in the brave new world of cloud native. Godspeed.

Index

© Mainak Chakraborty and Ajit Pratap Kundan 2021
M. Chakraborty and A. P. Kundan, *Monitoring Cloud-Native Applications*,
https://doi.org/10.1007/978-1-4842-6888-9

Printed in the United States
by Baker & Taylor Publisher Services